Windows XP® and Office 2003
Keyboard Shortcuts

Guy Hart-Davis

D0107455

McGraw-Hill/Osborne
New York Chicago San Francisco
Lisbon London Madrid Mexico City
Milan New Delhi San Juan
Seoul Singapore Sydney Toronto

The McGraw·Hill Companies

McGraw-Hill/Osborne
2100 Powell Street, 10th Floor
Emeryville, California 94608
U.S.A.

To arrange bulk purchase discounts for sales promotions, premiums, or fund-raisers, please contact **McGraw-Hill**/Osborne at the above address. For information on translations or book distributors outside the U.S.A., please see the International Contact Information page immediately following the index of this book.

Windows XP® and Office 2003 Keyboard Shortcuts

1234567890 DOC DOC 01987654

ISBN 0-07-225500-5

Publisher	**Copy Editor**
Brandon A. Nordin	Judith Brown
Vice President &	**Proofreader**
Associate Publisher	Paul Tyler
Scott Rogers	**Indexer**
Editorial Director	Claire Splan
Roger Stewart	**Composition**
Project Editor	Carie Abrew, Lucie Ericksen,
Madhu Prasher	Dick Schwartz
Acquisitions Coordinator	**Illustrators**
Agatha Kim	Kathleen Edwards, Melinda Lytle
Technical Editor	**Series Design**
Kim Frank	Dick Schwartz, Peter F. Hancik

This book was composed with Corel VENTURA™ Publisher.

Contents

Need to get your work done quickly and accurately with Windows XP and Office? Then use the keyboard more.

The mouse is great for precise graphical operations, but for invoking commands quickly and accurately, the keyboard rules. This book shows you how to make the most of your keyboard by using the keyboard shortcuts built into Windows XP and Office—and by creating your own keyboard shortcuts to supplement those built in.

Who Is This Book For?

This book is for users of Windows XP and Office who want to get their work done more quickly, accurately, and efficiently. That probably means *you*. Unless you find yourself spending large chunks of your workday staring into space or drumming your fingers to the latest beats while waiting for more work to show up, you can benefit from saving time and effort by using keyboard shortcuts.

This book assumes that you're familiar with the basics of the applications you're using, and that you want to use them more efficiently. For example, this book assumes that you know how to start Windows XP, log on and off, run applications, use Windows Explorer, and perform basic file management. Similarly, this book doesn't tell you what a Word document or an Excel worksheet *is*, but rather how to create and work in documents and worksheets faster and more efficiently.

If you're looking for a general introduction to Windows XP and Office 2003, consider larger and fuller books such as *Windows XP Home Edition: The Complete Reference*, *Windows XP Professional: The Complete Reference*, and *Office 2003: The Complete Reference*, all published by Osborne.

What Does This Book Cover?

This book explains how to use keyboard shortcuts in Windows XP and the Office 2003 applications: Word, Excel, PowerPoint, Outlook, and Access. Most of the keyboard shortcuts in Office 2003 apply to Office XP (aka Office 2002) and Office 2000 as well. This book points out the major differences that you'll need to know about if you use Office XP or Office 2000 instead of Office 2003.

》 Note: *Unless otherwise noted, the screens shown are from Office 2003, on the basis that this is the latest and most capable version of Office and the one you're most likely to be using, either now or eventually.*

The book's coverage is arranged by application and by topic. Within each topic, you'll learn the keyboard shortcuts you need in order to perform essential actions swiftly without reaching for your mouse.

Besides telling you how to use, customize, and create keyboard shortcuts, this book also tells you how to choose the best keyboard for your needs and your budget and how to configure it. To keep prices down, computer vendors typically provide only the most basic of keyboards with computers, so you could probably benefit from upgrading your keyboard if you haven't done so already. This book explains the range of keyboards available, from conventional keyboards to one-handed keyboards and keyless keyboards, and explains how to configure your keyboard for comfort and speed. The trinity of keyboard, mouse, and monitor largely govern how comfortable your computer use is—and there's no sense in being less comfortable than you need to be, even if you're not yet suffering from RSI.

Conventions Used in This Book

This book uses the following conventions to make the text easy to follow:

- Key caps such as ⊞-Break represent keyboard shortcuts. Hyphens mean that you should press the keys in combination.

- Multiple key caps in sequence separated by commas (for example, Ctrl-F6, Shift-F6) indicate shortcuts that are alternatives to each other. To indicate a sequence, this book uses the word "then": for example, Ctrl-Esc, then R.

- The | symbol represents making a choice from a menu. For example, "choose File | Print" means that you should open the File menu and choose the Print command from it. (Usually, you'll press Ctrl-P instead, because it's quicker.)

Keyboard Basics—and How to Enhance Your Keyboard

You'd be hard put to find a computer user who doesn't know what a keyboard is, but it would probably be nearly as difficult to find a computer user who uses the keyboard to the max. This chapter shows you how to configure your keyboard as well as possible and use such accessibility options as may help you. The chapter starts by making sure you know your way around your keyboard and the correct way to press keyboard shortcuts. After all, there's no point in getting the basics wrong.

>> **Note:** *You might also benefit from upgrading to a better keyboard. The appendix discusses the different types of keyboards available and suggests how to choose among them.*

Understanding the Standard Keys

A standard PC keyboard (Figure 1-1) contains 101 or 104 keys that break down as follows:

- Twenty-six letter keys for the letters a through z.

- A ⌞Spacebar⌟ to put spaces between characters.

- Two sets of keys for the single-digit numbers (0 through 9), one set appearing as a row above the letter keys and one set on the numeric keypad. The row of number keys double as symbol keys, and the numeric keypad keys double as navigation keys.

- Fifteen to 18 keys for mainstream punctuation symbols (for example, comma, period, and semicolon) and other symbols (for example, + and ~). The numeric keypad typically includes symbols used for basic mathematical operations (+ for addition, – for subtraction, / for division, and * for multiplication) and a period for a decimal place.

- A (Tab) key for entering tabs and for navigating from one interface element to another.

- Two (Enter) keys for entering carriage returns and "clicking" the selected button in dialog boxes.

- Two (Shift) keys to change the case of the key pressed, and a (Caps Lock) key to lock the letter keys in the capital position.

- Six other modifier keys: two (Ctrl) keys, two (Alt) keys, and two (⊞) buttons (discussed in the next section).

- An (Insert) key for toggling Insert mode.

- A (Delete) key for deleting the selection or the character after the insertion point, and a (Backspace) key for deleting the character before the insertion point.

- Eight or more navigation keys: four arrow keys ((←), (→), (↑), and (↓)), a (Home) key for moving to the beginning of an item, an (End) key for moving to the end of an item, a (Page Up) key for moving up by a "page" of information, and a (Page Down) key for moving down by a page.

- Twelve function keys, numbered (F1) to (F12), for invoking functionality built into the operating system and into applications.

- A (Scroll Lock) key that toggles the locking on the scrolling function.

- A (Num Lock) key for locking on the numeric keypad.

- A (Print Screen) (or (PrtScr)) key for capturing what appears on screen.

- A (Pause/Break) key for special functions.

- An (Esc) key for canceling an action or "clicking" the Cancel button in a dialog box.

- A context menu key (or shortcut menu key) for displaying the context menu or shortcut menu.

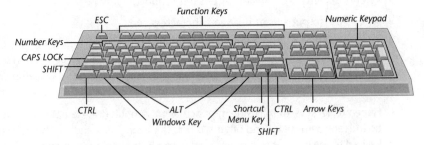

Figure 1-1   *A standard 104-key keyboard layout*

Using the Modifier Keys

The standard keys discussed in the previous section are mostly easy enough to use: to get an *a*, you press the Ⓐ key; to get a 1, you press the ①key; and so on. To use a keyboard shortcut, you typically press one of the *modifier keys—* keys that modify the effect of the key you press. (That sentence says "typically" because a few keyboard shortcuts don't use any modifier key, as you'll see later in this book.)

Standard keyboards for Windows PCs include four modifier keys (Figure 1-2):

- Ⓢʰⁱᶠᵗ The Ⓢʰⁱᶠᵗ key derives from the typewriter and changes the case of the letter. The name comes from the Ⓢʰⁱᶠᵗ key on a typewriter physically shifting the typewriter mechanism—either lifting the platen or lowering the typebars so that the top part of the typebar (containing the uppercase letter), rather than the lower part of the typebar (containing the lowercase letter), strikes the platen. (The *typebars* are the metal bars containing the letters. The *platen* is the roller around which the sheet of paper is wrapped and fed, and against which the typebars strike.)

- Ⓐˡᵗ The Ⓐˡᵗ key alters the keypress. In Windows, Ⓐˡᵗ is used to access accelerator keys on menus and other command bars (such as toolbars). For example, to display the File menu in many applications, you press Ⓐˡᵗ-Ⓕ.

- Ⓒᵗʳˡ The Ⓒᵗʳˡ key (pronounced "control") is used in Windows to trigger keyboard shortcuts. For example, to issue a Print command in many applications, you can press Ⓒᵗʳˡ-Ⓟ.

- ⊞ The ⊞ key is used for shortcuts that involve Windows itself rather than the applications that run on it. For example, you can press ⊞-Ⓡ to display the Run dialog box or ⊞-Ⓑʳᵉᵃᵏ to display the System Properties dialog box.

Ⓒᵗʳˡ, Ⓐˡᵗ, and Ⓢʰⁱᶠᵗ can be used in combination, thus producing many more key combinations—for example, Ⓒᵗʳˡ-Ⓜ, Ⓒᵗʳˡ-Ⓐˡᵗ-Ⓜ, Ⓒᵗʳˡ-Ⓐˡᵗ-Ⓢʰⁱᶠᵗ-Ⓜ, Ⓒᵗʳˡ-Ⓢʰⁱᶠᵗ-Ⓜ, and Ⓐˡᵗ-Ⓢʰⁱᶠᵗ-Ⓜ. The more keys in a combination, the harder it is for most users to press, but the less chance that any user will press that combination by

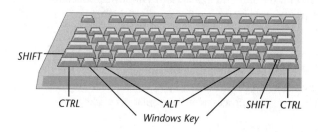

Figure 1-2
Standard PC keyboards have four modifier keys: Ⓢʰⁱᶠᵗ, Ⓐˡᵗ, Ⓒᵗʳˡ, and ⊞.

SHIFT

CTRL · ALT · SHIFT · CTRL

Windows Key

accident. ⊞ isn't normally used in combination with other modifier keys, although it is possible to program Windows to recognize such key combinations.

Many laptops include another modifier key on their keyboard: the function (Fn) key, which is typically used to provide additional functionality on a keyboard that doesn't have enough keys for each separate function. For example, pressing Fn-F5 on some laptops decreases the screen brightness, and Fn-F6 increases it.

 A laptop keyboard may also have an embedded keypad to provide the functionality of the keypad on a full-size keyboard. The embedded keypad usually appears on the right-hand side of the keyboard, with the letter J doubling for 1, K for 2, and L for 3. You press a numeric lock key (NumLock) to activate the keypad function.

Pressing Key Combinations

To use a key combination, you typically hold down the modifier key or keys while you press the alphanumeric key. For example, to issue a Print command, you press Ctrl and hold it down, press and release P, and then release Ctrl. To press Ctrl-Shift-M, you press and hold down Ctrl and Shift together while you press M.

Alt works this way as well, either in combinations or on its own, but you can also press Alt and release it before pressing the alphanumeric key. Pressing the Alt key makes Windows put the focus on the first item in the menu bar, which is typically the File menu. When you press the *access key* (the underlined letter), Windows activates that menu. For example, when you press W, Windows activates the Window menu in many applications.

Once the menu is open, you can invoke a command on it by pressing the command's access key without pressing Alt again. In many applications, most of the frequently used commands have access keys. But because each access key needs to be unique for best effect, some less frequently used commands have either no access key or an unintuitive access key.

Access keys are also known as *mnemonics* because they frequently use the beginning letter or a key letter of the command. For example, the access key for the Save command on the File menu in standard Windows applications is *S* (the first letter), and the access key for the Exit command is *X* (the first sound in the word *exit*).

If two or more commands on the same menu use the same access key, press the key once to select the first command; then press again to select the next command. When you've reached the command you want, press Enter to invoke it. Figure 1-3 illustrates the process with a regular access key.

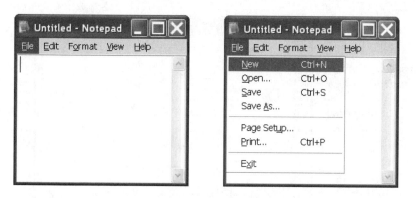

Figure 1-3   *Using an* Alt *keyboard shortcut most effectively: press* Alt *to activate the first item on the menu bar (left), press the access key to display the menu (right), and then press the access key for the command.*

Configuring Your Keyboard

Windows XP ships with default keyboard settings that work tolerably well for many people. But to get the best results from your keyboard, you may need to configure it.

Windows XP supports three different types of configuration settings:

- **Basic keyboard settings** You can configure the speed and delay for repeating characters, and the speed at which the cursor (the insertion point) blinks.

- **Keyboard layouts** You can change the logical layout of your physical keyboard to one of a number of alternative layouts.

- **Accessibility features** You can use special accessibility features that Windows XP offers to make your keyboard easier to use.

If these three types of configuration settings don't give you the results you need, you may want to get a different keyboard. I discuss your options in the appendix.

Changing Basic Keyboard Settings

Your first option is to change the rate at which the cursor blinks and the rate at which Windows XP repeats characters when you keep a key pressed down. To configure these options, choose Start | Control Panel | Printers and Other Hardware | Keyboard, and work in the Keyboard Properties dialog box (Figure 1-4).

>> Note: *If you're using Classic view of Control Panel rather than Category view, choose Start | Control Panel, and then double-click the Keyboard icon. To switch between Category view and Classic view, click the Switch to Classic View link or the Switch to Category View link in the Control Panel task pane.*

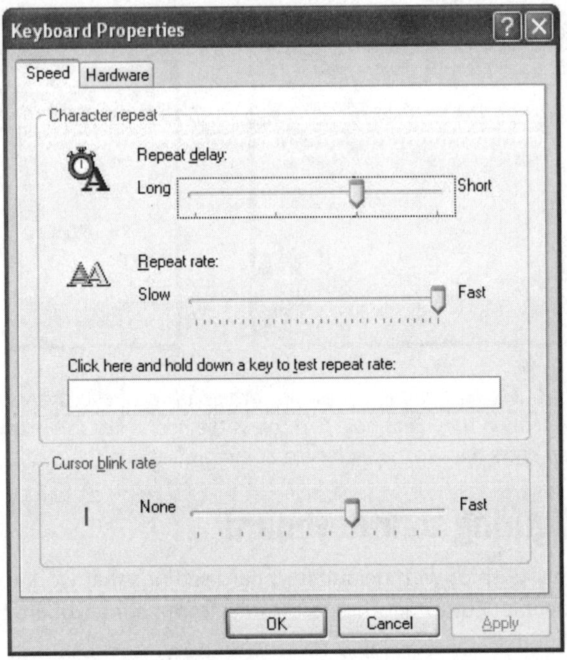

Figure 1-4
You can change
your keyboard's
repeat rate and the
cursor blink rate in
the Keyboard
Properties
dialog box.

Using Keyboard Accessibility Features

If you find it difficult to press key combinations consistently, you may be able to improve matters by using Windows' keyboard accessibility features. These features are designed to help Windows users who have mild to moderate disabilities, but no disability is required—if you're able bodied, and you find an accessibility feature useful, go ahead and use it. It's not like parking in a Disabled space.

Choose Start | Control Panel to open a Control Panel window, and then click the Accessibility Options icon to display the Accessibility Options screen. Click the Accessibility Options icon again to display the Accessibility Options dialog box. If the Keyboard tab (Figure 1-5) isn't displayed, click the tab to display its controls.

The Keyboard tab offers three keyboard enhancements: StickyKeys, FilterKeys, and ToggleKeys. You can turn these enhancements on or off by selecting or clearing the Use StickyKeys check box, the Use FilterKeys check box, and the Use ToggleKeys check box on the Keyboard tab of the Accessibility Options dialog box. Each of the enhancements has configuration options that you can set by clicking the Settings button in its area and working in the resulting Settings dialog box. Most of the Settings dialog boxes offer a test area so that you can see how the current settings suit you.

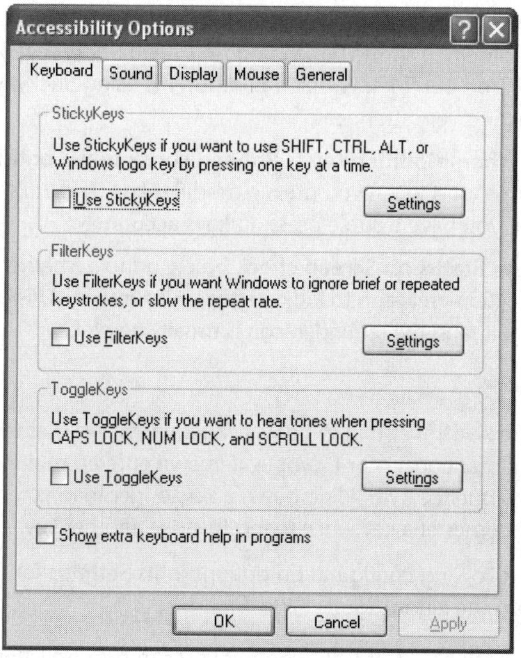

Figure 1-5
*Windows'
StickyKeys,
FilterKeys, and
ToggleKeys
options can make
keyboard shortcuts
easier to press
consistently.*

StickyKeys

StickyKeys enables you to "stick" the modifier keys on so that you can press them one at a time (for example, Alt, then Shift, then F1) instead of having to press them all together. To turn StickyKeys on, you press Shift five times in succession. To turn StickyKeys off, double-click the StickyKeys icon in the notification area to display the Accessibility Options dialog box, clear the Use StickyKeys check box, and then click the OK button. (If you turn off the StickyKeys notification area icon, display the Accessibility Options dialog box from Control Panel.)

StickyKeys offers the following configuration options in its Settings for StickyKeys dialog box (Figure 1-6):

- **Use Shortcut check box**   Controls whether you can turn StickyKeys on by pressing Shift five times in succession.

- **Press Modifier Key Twice to Lock check box**   Controls whether Windows locks the modifier key on when you press it twice in succession. For example, press Ctrl twice to lock it on so that you can invoke two or more Ctrl keyboard shortcuts without pressing Ctrl. Press the same modifier key again to unlock it.

- **Turn StickyKeys Off if Two Keys Are Pressed at Once check box**   Controls whether Windows turns StickyKeys off when someone presses two keys together—in other words, when someone invokes a keyboard shortcut the normal way. This option, which is turned on by default, is intended to make StickyKeys turn off when someone who doesn't need StickyKeys starts using the computer. If you don't know that a computer is using StickyKeys, you may think it's acting very strangely.

- **Make Sounds When Modifier Key Is Pressed check box** Controls whether Windows plays a sound when you press a modifier key. This aural feedback can be helpful if you have trouble pressing keys accurately.

- **Show StickyKeys Status on Screen check box** Controls whether StickyKeys displays a notification-area icon to indicate that it is running. This check box is selected by default, and the reminder icon is usually helpful.

FilterKeys

FilterKeys analyzes the keystrokes that Windows experiences and tries to determine which of them are unintentional—for example, if you've entered multiple instances of the same letter in sequence by holding down a key longer than you needed to, or if you blipped the corner of a key while trying to strike another key.

FilterKeys offers the following configuration options in its Settings for FilterKeys dialog box (shown on the left in Figure 1-7):

- **Use Shortcut check box** Controls whether you can turn on FilterKeys by holding down Shift for eight seconds.

- **Filter Options area** Select the Ignore Repeated Keystrokes option button or the "Ignore Quick Keystrokes and Slow Down the Repeat Rate" option button, as appropriate. If you select the Ignore Repeated Keystrokes option button, click the Settings button and specify the minimum keystroke

Figure 1-6
Configure StickyKeys' behavior in the Settings for StickyKeys dialog box.

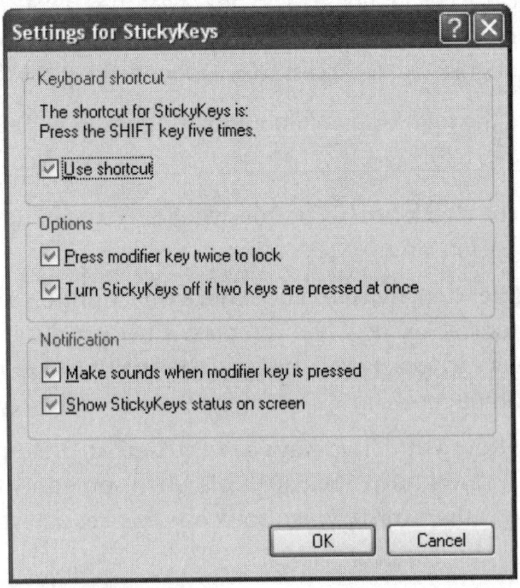

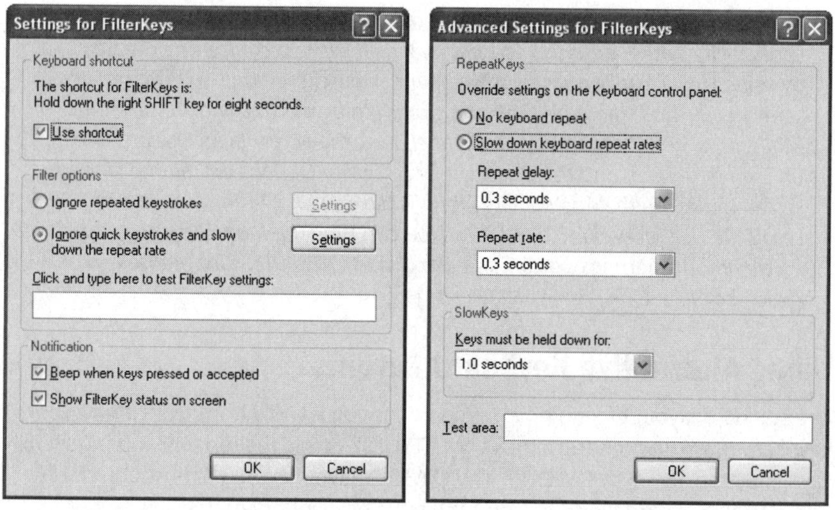

Figure 1-7   *FilterKeys (left) filters out repeated and misstruck keystrokes from your typing. Use the Advanced Settings for FilterKeys dialog box (right) to configure settings for ignoring quick keystrokes and slowing down the keyboard repeat rate.*

interval (from 0.5 second to 2 seconds) in the Advanced Settings for FilterKeys dialog box. If you select the "Ignore Quick Keystrokes and Slow Down the Repeat Rate" option button, click the Settings button and choose RepeatKeys (repeating keys) and SlowKeys (minimum-length keypresses) in the Advanced Settings for FilterKeys dialog box (shown on the right in Figure 1-7).

- **Notification area** By default, both the Beep When Keys Pressed or Accepted check box and the Show FilterKey Status on Screen check box are selected. Clear these check boxes if you don't find the feedback helpful. As with StickyKeys, a visual reminder tends to be useful because a computer with FilterKeys active can appear to be acting very strangely—for example, you can type whole sentences and not register a single key if you're not holding down the keys long enough for SlowKeys.

ToggleKeys

ToggleKeys makes Windows play tones when you press (Caps Lock), (Num Lock), or (Scroll Lock). ToggleKeys can be useful even for full-speed typists who may strike these keys by accident as they go for other keys. Some advanced keyboards also play warning tones to let you know that you've pressed these keys.

The only configuration option for ToggleKeys is the Use Shortcut check box, which controls whether you can turn ToggleKeys on from the keyboard by holding down (Num Lock) for five seconds.

>> *Tip:* *If you want to use your keyboard as much as possible, another accessibility option to try is MouseKeys, which lets you control the mouse by using the arrow keys on your keyboard. MouseKeys don't suit everybody: some people find them too slow and clumsy to be worth using. To turn on MouseKeys, choose Start | Control Panel, click the Accessibility Options link on the first screen, and then click the Accessibility Options link on the second screen to display the Accessibility Options dialog box. On the Mouse tab, select the Use MouseKeys check box. You can tune the MouseKeys settings by clicking the Settings button and working in the Settings for MouseKeys dialog box.*

Using Alternative Keyboard Layouts

The standard layout of keys on a keyboard, as you'll know from glancing at your keyboard every day, has the letters QWERTYUIOP across the top row and is generally known by the acronym QWERTY. The QWERTY layout is used almost universally in the English-typing world but isn't the most efficient or comfortable layout for extended typing.

QWERTY was designed in the 1870s by Christopher Latham Sholes, the leading inventor of the first typewriter produced in commercial quantities. The prime consideration influencing the layout was the need to prevent the keybars from jamming when the user was typing fast, but commercial considerations were also involved: Sholes included all the letters for the word *typewriter* in the top line so that his salesmen could type it more easily when demonstrating the typewriter. The result was that only about 36 percent of the letters you type on a QWERTY keyboard are on the home row, so your fingers have to move frequently to the other rows of keys.

As you'll probably agree from your experience of learning to type, the QWERTY layout isn't easy to learn; if you use it extensively, you may also agree that it's not efficient to use either. But because it became the standard layout relatively quickly after its introduction, and because it has remained the standard layout in the English-typing world, QWERTY has such a lock on the market that no alternative keyboard layout has gained much traction. Not surprisingly, few people want to learn to type again, and QWERTY works well enough once you've learned it, so it seems likely to be with us to stay.

The keyboard layout is hard-coded into a typewriter, so to change the letter that a key delivered, you'd need to saw the keybar off and weld on a different one. With computers, making changes is much easier. The physical layout of the keyboard is hard-coded, although with some keyboards, you can pop off the key caps (the caps that constitute the physical keys) and slide them back on in different places if you choose. (This works only for standard keyboards.) But the logical layout can be changed either on the keyboard or on the computer with minimal effort. Should you want to try a different keyboard layout, you need only tell your keyboard or your computer so.

Which Layout Should You Use?

At this point, you're probably not too excited about the possibilities of logical layouts unless you have a particular logical layout in mind. After all, to use a different layout, you either need to buy a keyboard that has that layout, physically customize your keyboard to show that layout (for example, by rearranging the key caps or pasting stickers over the letters on them), or touch-type on a keyboard whose keys show different letters than they deliver. (You should be touch-typing in any case, because doing so saves you a huge amount of time and effort over looking for the keys. But even so, having each key produce a different letter than it bears can be disconcerting, especially when you're trying to type passwords and can't see on screen which letters you're getting.)

For most people, the primary alternative is one of the implementations of the Dvorak keyboard layout—for example, the United States-Dvorak layout that comes built into Windows XP. Unlike QWERTY, the Dvorak layout was designed for efficient typing in English, and in typical use, about 74 percent of keystrokes are on the home row, so your fingers needn't move nearly as far as with QWERTY. August Dvorak, the inventor of the Dvorak layout, also laid out the keys to use as much as possible the hand's natural drumming rhythm from pinkie to index finger.

The Dvorak layout has many enthusiasts (full disclosure: I'm one) but has barely scratched the surface of the mainstream typing market because QWERTY, as the default keyboard format, has the market pretty thoroughly sewn up. You can buy keyboards with Dvorak layouts from specialist keyboard retailers, but the easiest way to get started is to download a Dvorak key chart from the Internet, apply the Windows XP United States-Dvorak keyboard layout (using the technique discussed next), and learn to touch-type with it.

Dvorak's far from the only option: Windows XP supports an impressive array of different keyboard layouts, as you can see in the Add Input Language dialog box (which you'll meet in a moment). But unless you learned to type on a particular keyboard layout, or a layout offers better key placement for particular keys you find difficult to press, you won't usually have a strong reason for choosing it over your existing keyboard layout.

Applying a Different Keyboard Layout

To apply a different keyboard layout, follow these steps:

1. Choose Start | Control Panel to display Control Panel.

2. Click the Date, Time, Language, and Regional Options item to display the Date, Time, Language, and Regional Options screen.

3. Click the Regional and Language Options item to display the Regional and Language Options dialog box.

4. Click the Languages tab to display its contents.

5. In the Text Services and Input Languages group box, click the Details button to display the Text Services and Input Languages dialog box.

6. Click the Add button to display the Add Input Language dialog box:

Add Input language   ? X

Input language:
English (United States)

Keyboard layout/IME:
United States-Dvorak

OK   Cancel

7. In the Input Language drop-down list, select the input language if necessary. (For some keyboard layouts, you can simply leave your current input language selected.)

8. In the Keyboard Layout/IME drop-down list, select the keyboard layout you want to use. For example, select the United States-Dvorak layout to use the Dvorak layout with a standard U.S. keyboard.

9. Click the OK button to close the Add Input Language dialog box and add the layout to the list in the Installed Services list box.

10. Add further layouts as necessary by repeating steps 6 through 9.

11. Click the OK button to close the Text Services and Input Languages dialog box.

12. Click the OK button to close the Regional and Language Options dialog box.

13. Click the close button (the × button) to close the Date, Time, Language, and Regional Options dialog box.

Switching Among Keyboard Layouts

When you add a second keyboard layout to Windows XP, Windows XP automatically displays the Language bar so that you can easily switch from one layout to another. Depending on your settings, the Language bar may appear either as a free-floating bar over your applications or on the taskbar just to the left of the notification area. Either way, you can switch from one layout to another by clicking the Keyboard icon and choosing the layout from the resulting menu.

English (United States)   ?
✓ English (United States)
United States-Dvorak

Given that we're talking about keyboard shortcuts in this book, you may prefer to switch among keyboard layouts by using keyboard shortcuts rather than the mouse. To set your computer up to do so, follow these steps:

1. Right-click the Language bar or the taskbar icon, and choose Settings from the shortcut menu to display the Text Services and Input Languages dialog box. When you display the dialog box this way, it contains only the Settings tab, but otherwise it's the same as shown in Figure 1-8, earlier in this chapter.

2. Click the Key Settings button to display the Advanced Key Settings dialog box:

Advanced Key Settings

To turn off Caps Lock
- ⦿ Press the CAPS LOCK key   ○ Press the SHIFT key

Hot keys for input languages

Action	Key sequence
Switch between input languages	Left Alt+Shift
Switch to English (United States) - United States-Dvorak	(None)
Switch to English (United States) - US	(None)

Change Key Sequence...

OK   Cancel

3. In the Hot Keys for Input Languages group box, select the item for which you want to set the key sequence:

- This group box contains a Switch Between Input Languages item that switches to the next keyboard layout, and a Switch To item for each input language and keyboard layout—for example, "Switch to English (United States) - United States-Dvorak" for the United States-Dvorak keyboard layout using U.S. English.

- The Switch Between Input Languages item is set by default to ⌜Left Alt⌝-⌜Shift⌝. Note that ⌜Left Alt⌝ is ⌜Alt⌝ on the left of the keyboard, not ⌜←⌝-⌜Alt⌝.

4. Click the Change Key Sequence button to display the Change Key Sequence dialog box:

Change Key Sequence

Switch to English (United States) - United States-Dvorak
☑ Enable Key Sequence
- ○ CTRL   + SHIFT + Key: 0
- ⦿ Left ALT

OK   Cancel

5. Select the Enable Key Sequence check box if it's not already selected.

6. Select the Ctrl option button to create a keyboard shortcut using ⌞Ctrl⌟-⌞Shift⌟ or the Alt option button to create a shortcut using ⌞Alt⌟-⌞Shift⌟.

7. In the Key drop-down list, select the number key to use for the keyboard shortcut. You can also select the tilde key (~) or the grave accent key (`) if you prefer.

8. Click the OK button to close the Change Key Sequence dialog box. Windows XP adds the new keyboard shortcut to the list in the Advanced Key Settings dialog box.

9. Repeat steps 3 through 8 to create keyboard shortcuts for as many of your other keyboard layouts as you want.

10. Click the OK button to close the Advanced Key Settings dialog box.

11. Click the OK button to close the Text Services and Input Languages dialog box.

You can then switch to a different keyboard layout by pressing the keyboard shortcut you chose for it. Alternatively, press the Switch Between Input Languages keyboard shortcut to cycle through your keyboard layouts.

Switching the Language Bar Between Docked and Floating

To dock the Language bar from its free-floating state, right-click it and choose Minimize from the shortcut menu. Windows XP displays a Language bar message box to make sure you know what you've done. Select the Don't Show Me This Message Again check box, and click the OK button to close the message box.

To undock the Language bar, right-click it and choose Restore the Language Bar from the shortcut menu.

Configuring How the Language Bar Appears

To configure how the Language bar appears, or to turn it off, follow these steps:

1. Right-click the Language bar or the taskbar icon and choose Settings from the shortcut menu to display the Text Services and Input Languages dialog box.

2. Click the Language Bar button to display the Language Bar Settings dialog box:

3. Choose settings as appropriate:

- Select the Show the Language Bar on the Desktop check box to display the Language bar.

- Select the Show the Language Bar as Transparent When Inactive check box if you want Windows to make the Language bar transparent when you're not actively using it. This check box is available only when the Language bar is floating, not when it is docked on the taskbar.

- Select the Show Additional Language Bar Icons in the Notification Area check box if you want to display all the Language bar icons in the taskbar. (Depending on your configuration of Windows XP and Office, this check box may be called "Show Additional Language Bar Icons in the Taskbar.")

- Select the Show Text Labels on the Language Bar check box if you want to display text labels as well as icons on the Language bar. Text labels make the buttons more comprehensible, but they take up more space. This check box is available only when the Language bar is floating, not when it is docked on the taskbar.

- Select or clear the Turn Off Advanced Text Services check box to control whether text services such as speech recognition and handwriting recognition are turned on or off. If you're not using these features, clear this check box.

4. Click the OK button to close the Language Bar Settings dialog box.

5. Click the OK button to clear the Text Services and Input Languages dialog box.

Using Remapping Utilities to Remap the Keys on Your Keyboard

By this point, you should have your keyboard pretty well configured. But there's one more option you should be aware of: you can remap the keys on your keyboard so that they produce different keystrokes than normal for the keyboard layout you're using.

This is where it gets a little weird. With a standard keyboard layout, such as U.S. English, you'll get the letter for the key you press: press Ⓒ, you get a c, and so on. If you've applied a different keyboard layout, such as Dvorak, you'll get a different letter for that same key: press Ⓒ, and you get a j, because that's where the j is in the Dvorak layout. But even with a different keyboard layout applied, you can remap any given key so that it produces a different keystroke yet.

Fair enough, you may be saying—but why would you want to remap a key from your chosen layout? The usual reason is to work around a marginally abnormal layout that the manufacturer has designed into your laptop. For example, for years Toshiba designed its laptop keyboards with only one [Alt] key, which was positioned in the regular location for the left [Alt] key. Anyone used to using the right [Alt] key was straight out of luck if they or their company bought a Toshiba laptop. But with a remapping utility, they could make the key Toshiba put in the right [Alt] position into an [Alt] key, thus saving time and temper. Similarly, some people like to swap the positions of [Ctrl] and [Caps Lock] on their keys to make typing easier.

To remap the keys, you use a remapping utility. If you search on the Web, you'll find various remapping utilities. Some are free, having been written by disgruntled keyboard users who choose to share the fruits of their labors. Others cost a few dollars. At this writing, one of the best freeware remappers for Windows XP is Travis Krumsick's KeyTweak, which you can download from **http://webpages .charter.net/krumsick/**. KeyTweak has a straightforward interface in which you specify which physical key to remap, which logical key to remap it to, and then commit the changes.

Remapping Your Keyboard Physically

Logical remapping is one thing, physical remapping another. If you apply a different keyboard layout, or remap keys logically by using a remapping utility, you'll end up with keys that produce a different letter from that shown on the key caps. If you're touch-typing, that may not be too much of a problem, but you may still be tempted to improve matters.

With some keyboards, you can pop off the key caps and put them back on in different positions without doing any damage. With others, you'll find that some keys fit only in certain positions, and that you can't change the layout of the key caps physically. In this case, your best bet is to apply stickers neatly over the keys you've changed.

Cubeboard Ltd. (**www.personalkeyboard.com**) has announced keyboards (and other products, such as remote controls) in which you can easily remove and rearrange the keys. Better yet, each key cap is hard-coded to its characters, so it "knows" which letter to produce; when you move the key cap to a different position on the keyboard, it still delivers the same letter, so you don't need to apply a different logical layout or remap keys.

Cubeboard's plans sound great, but at this writing, Cubeboard hasn't brought its products to market.

2

Windows XP and Windows Explorer Keyboard Shortcuts

Your first step toward using more keyboard shortcuts should be to master those built into Windows XP itself and the most important applications and applets that come with it. This chapter sets you on your way by discussing shortcuts for Windows XP and Windows Explorer.

Working with Windows XP

As you and your mouse know all too well, Windows XP is a graphical operating system, and in many cases, the mouse is the easiest way to take actions quickly. But Windows XP does support various keyboard shortcuts, and it pays to know them—particularly those dozen or so involving ⊞.

Windows Key Shortcuts

The quickest way to take a variety of common actions in Windows XP is to use the keyboard shortcuts that use ⊞.

⊞

Display or hide the Start menu

Pressing ⊞ is equivalent to clicking the Start button. Press ⊞ again to toggle the Start menu off. You can then navigate the Start menu by using the arrow keys or by typing the starting letter of each item you want to move to.

Ctrl-Esc

Display or hide the Start menu

This shortcut is an alternative to pressing ⊞ (or clicking the Start button). It's most useful on keyboards that don't have ⊞ or if you find ⊞ hard to press without striking another key.

⊞-B

Move the focus to the notification area

Because the notification area is graphical, it's usually easier to use the mouse to manipulate it. But this shortcut can be useful if you have mouse problems.

⊞-Break

Display the System Properties dialog box

The System Properties dialog box (Figure 2-1) contains seven tabs of information and controls for checking and working with your computer's hardware. (If you're using Windows XP Professional, an administrator may have prevented one or more tabs from appearing so that you can't make changes on them.) You can also display the System Properties dialog box by right-clicking the My Computer item on the Start menu and choosing Properties from the shortcut menu.

⊞-D

Perform a Show the Desktop command

The Show the Desktop command minimizes all open windows and dialog boxes so that you can see your desktop (for example, to access files on it).

⊞-E

Open a My Computer window in Windows Explorer

The My Computer window gives you quick access to your computer's drives, the Shared Documents folder, and your My Documents folder (which appears as

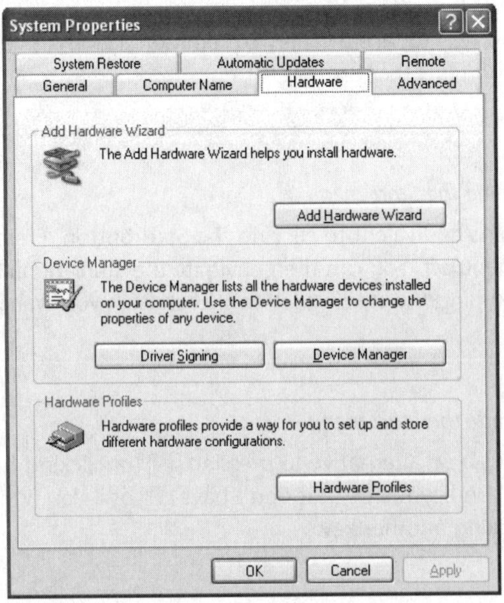

Figure 2-1
Press ⊞-Break to instantly display the System Properties dialog box.

Username's Documents, where *Username* is your Windows user name, rather than My Documents).

⊞-F

Open a Search Results window in Windows Explorer and launch Search Companion

Use this shortcut to quickly open a Search window from the keyboard.

⊞-Ctrl-F

Open a Search Results window in Windows Explorer and launch Search Companion in Search for Computer mode

Use this awkward shortcut when you need to search for a computer on the network.

⊞-F1

Open Help and Support Center

This shortcut is the equivalent of choosing Start | Help and Support.

⊞-L

Lock the computer

Press this shortcut to lock Windows XP and display either the Login screen or the Log On to Windows dialog box (depending on how Windows XP is configured).

⊞-M

Minimize all open windows

This useful shortcut minimizes all open windows to buttons on the taskbar, enabling you to see your desktop and its icons at a keystroke.

⊞-Shift-M

Restore minimized windows

Use this shortcut to restore the windows you've minimized by a ⊞-M command.

⊞-R

Display the Run dialog box

Use the Run dialog box (shown next) to quickly run an application, open a file, or access a web site. Type the application name, file name, or URL in the Open text box, and then click the OK button.

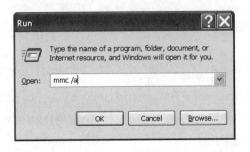

⊞-Tab

Move the focus to the next taskbar button

Use this shortcut one or more times to select the application you want, and then press Enter to activate the application. If you have Windows XP set to group similar taskbar buttons, Windows XP groups related buttons when the taskbar starts to become crowded. Press ⊞-Tab to select the group button, press ↑ to select the button for the window you want, and then press Enter to activate it.

⊞-Shift-Tab

Move the focus to the previous taskbar button

Use this shortcut one or more times to select the application you want, and then press Enter to activate the application.

⊞-U

Launch Utility Manager

Utility Manager (shown here) lets you control the Magnifier, Narrator, and On-Screen Keyboard accessibility utilities.

Adding Windows Key Shortcuts

If you find 🎛 shortcuts a quick way of taking actions in Windows, consider creating more 🎛 shortcuts. Windows XP itself doesn't let you create further 🎛 shortcuts directly, but you can create them by using third-party software.

One of the best utilities for creating 🎛 shortcuts is the freeware WinKey from Copernic Technologies Inc. (**www.copernic.com/winkey**). WinKey (Figure 2-2) comes with various 🎛 shortcuts already assigned (for example, 🎛-⟵ minimizes the active window, and 🎛-Ⓝ opens a Windows Explorer window to your Network Neighborhood). You can also define custom 🎛 shortcuts of your own.

Creating Keyboard Shortcuts to Run Applications

Starting an application from the Start menu or from a desktop shortcut is easy enough, but there's an even easier way: assign a keyboard shortcut to the application so that you can start it directly from the keyboard.

To assign a keyboard shortcut to an application, follow these steps:

1. If you don't already have a shortcut for the application on the Start menu or on the desktop, create one. (For example, navigate to the application and issue a Send To | Desktop (Create Shortcut) from the shortcut menu or the File menu.)

2. Right-click the shortcut on the Start menu or the desktop and choose Properties from the shortcut menu to display the shortcut's Properties dialog box.

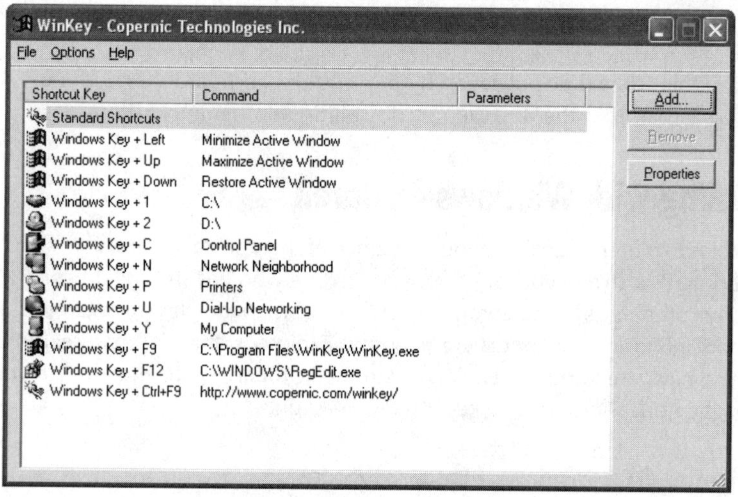

Figure 2-2   *The freeware utility WinKey lets you use further* 🎛 *shortcuts.*

3. Click the Shortcut tab (or press [Ctrl]-[Tab] one or more times) to display it if it's not already displayed:

4. Press [Alt]-[K] or click in the Shortcut Key text box.

5. Press the key you want to use for the keyboard shortcut. Windows XP automatically adds [Ctrl]-[Alt] to the shortcut, so if you press [w], Windows XP creates the shortcut [Ctrl]-[Alt]-[W] for the application.

6. Click the OK button to close the Properties dialog box.

You can then start the application by pressing the keyboard shortcut you applied, either from the desktop or from within another application.

Working with Windows Explorer

Windows Explorer appears the quintessence of a graphical application—and indeed that's a strong part of its appeal. Anyone who has struggled typing lengthy commands at the command prompt to manage files (for example, in DOS or Unix) tends to appreciate Windows Explorer's graphical nature. But you can also navigate Windows Explorer with the keyboard quite effectively if you know the right shortcuts and keypresses. Read on.

Navigating in a Windows Explorer Window

First, you'll need to know the keystrokes and shortcuts for navigating to the folder or file you want to affect.

[Backspace]

Move up to the parent folder

 Pressing [Backspace] is the equivalent of clicking the Up button on the Standard Buttons toolbar in Windows Explorer.

[F6]

Cycle through the screen elements in a window or on the desktop

Pressing [F6] moves the focus among the major screen elements in the active window. For example, in the Windows Explorer window shown in My Computer view in Figure 2-3, the Documents and Settings folder is selected. Pressing [F6] multiple times selects the following elements:

1. The Address bar
2. The Documents and Settings folder again
3. The System Tasks pane
4. The first item in the System Tasks pane
5. The File and Folder Tasks pane
6. The first item in the File and Folder Tasks pane
7. The Other Places pane
8. The first item in the Other Places pane
9. The Details pane
10. The Documents and Settings folder yet again (completing the cycle)

≫ Note: *If you have the Folders Explorer bar displayed rather than the task panes, pressing [F6] multiple times moves the selection among the current folder, the Address bar, and the Folders Explorer bar.*

[Enter] or **[Spacebar]**

Expand or collapse a task pane

When navigating using [F6] (or other means), select the heading of a task pane, and then press [Enter] or [Spacebar] to expand or collapse the task pane.

[Alt]-[D]

Select the address in the Address bar (when displayed)

If you use the Address bar to navigate from folder to folder, use this shortcut to quickly select the address in the Address bar so that you can type a new folder address or URL.

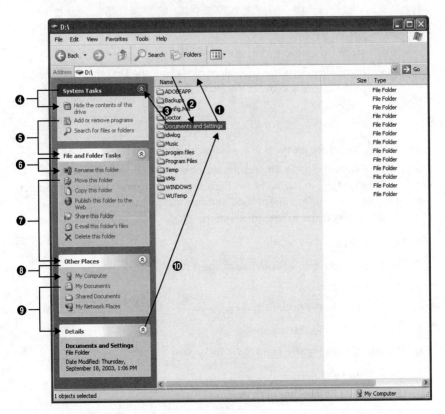

Figure 2-3   Pressing F6 cycles through the screen elements in a window. Here's the order for a Windows Explorer window with all its task panes displayed in My Computer view.

F4

Display the Address drop-down list in the Address bar

Use this shortcut to display the Address drop-down list so that you can use ↓ to select a local drive or folder from it. Alternatively, if you find the Alt-D keypress awkward, press F4 twice to select the address in the Address bar: the first press displays the drop-down list, and the second press collapses it, leaving it selected.

Tab

Move to the next control

←

Collapse the selected expanded folder, or select the parent folder

When navigating in a folder tree, press ⬅ to collapse an expanded folder that's currently selected. Once the folder is collapsed, pressing ⬅ selects the folder's parent folder.

➡

Expand the selected collapsed folder, or select the first subfolder in an expanded folder

When navigating in a folder tree, press ➡ to expand a collapsed folder that's currently selected. Once the folder is expanded, pressing ➡ selects the first subfolder contained in the folder.

➕ on the numeric keypad with (NumLock) on

Expand the selected collapsed folder

Pressing ➕ on the numeric keypad with (NumLock) switched on is the equivalent of clicking the + sign to expand a collapsed folder.

➖ on the numeric keypad with (NumLock) on

Collapse the selected expanded folder

Pressing ➖ on the numeric keypad with (NumLock) switched on is the equivalent of clicking the – sign to collapse an expanded folder.

(NumLock)-(*)

Display all of the subfolders that are under the selected folder

Instead of displaying just the next level of folders, you can display all subfolders by using this keyboard shortcut.

(End)

Scroll to the bottom of the active window

(Home)

Scroll to the top of the active window

(F3)

Display a Search Results window or Search Companion

Pressing (F3) from the desktop displays a Search Results window ready for searching. Pressing (F3) from a Windows Explorer window displays the Search Companion pane.

Windows XP & Windows Explorer

Alt - Enter

Display the Properties dialog box for the selected item or items

This shortcut works in a Windows Explorer window, from the desktop, and in common dialog boxes (such as the Open dialog box and the Save As dialog box).

Ctrl - A

Select all the items

This shortcut works in Windows Explorer and in most applications. In Windows Explorer, this shortcut selects all the objects in the folder. In Notepad or WordPad, this shortcut selects the entire contents of the document.

Shift - F10

Display the shortcut menu for the selected item

This shortcut has the same effect as right-clicking the item. Alternatively, if your keyboard includes a shortcut-menu key, you can press that key instead.

Copying, Cutting, or Pasting a File or Text

You can use Windows' Cut, Copy, and Paste commands to move or copy both files (and folders) and text.

Ctrl - C

Copy the selected text or object to the Clipboard

You can use this shortcut to copy the information about the selected files or folders, and then paste them by using a Paste command. If you have selected text within Windows Explorer (for example, part of a file name), this shortcut copies that text.

Ctrl - X

Cut the selected text or object to the Clipboard

Cutting an item removes it from its current location. You can use this shortcut as the first step in moving the selected files or folders. (To complete the move, issue a Paste command in the appropriate folder.) If you have selected text within Windows Explorer (for example, an address in the Address bar, or part of a file name), this shortcut cuts the text.

Ctrl - V

Paste the current object or text

You can use this shortcut to paste either files or text you've copied or cut. To paste files, open a Windows Explorer window to the destination folder, and then use this shortcut. To paste text into Windows Explorer, open an edit box, position the insertion point where you want the text inserted, and then use this shortcut. If the insertion point is collapsed (has no contents), Windows adds the item from the Clipboard. If the insertion point is a selection, Windows replaces the selection with the item you're pasting.

[Ctrl]-drag

Copy the item to the folder you drop it on

This shortcut works both in Windows Explorer and in most Windows applications.

[Ctrl]-[Shift]-drag

Create a shortcut to the dragged item

Hold down [Ctrl] and [Shift], and then drag the item from its source and drop it on your desktop or the folder you want to create the shortcut in.

[Ctrl]-[Z]

Undo the last action

In Windows Explorer, you can typically undo multiple actions that you've just taken. To see what the next undoable action is, display the Edit menu and check the top entry, which gives a brief explanation such as "Undo Move" or "Undo Rename."

Deleting and Moving to the Recycle Bin

The keyboard shortcuts for deleting files and moving files to the Recycle Bin are easy to remember, but it's worth being clear about exactly what happens when you use them.

[Delete]

Delete the selection

By default, when you delete a file or folder, Windows confirms that you want to move it to the Recycle Bin (as shown here), and then moves the file there.

Confirm File Delete

Are you sure you want to send 'The United States of America - Where Is Yesterday.mp3' to the Recycle Bin?

Yes   No

Windows XP & Windows Explorer

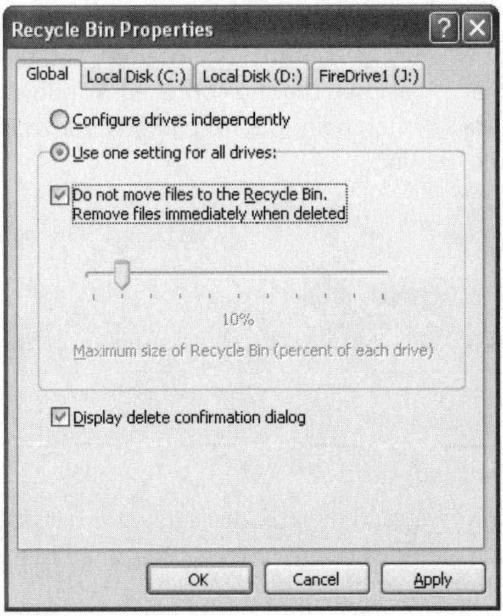

Figure 2-4

Select the "Do Not Move Files to the Recycle Bin. Remove Files Immediately When Deleted" check box to delete files and folders immediately.

To make Windows delete files immediately without moving them to the Recycle Bin, right-click the Recycle Bin icon on your desktop and choose Properties from the shortcut menu to display the Recycle Bin Properties dialog box (Figure 2-4). Select the "Do Not Move Files to the Recycle Bin. Remove Files Immediately When Deleted" check box on the Global tab (to affect all drives) or on the tab for the drive you want to affect.

Shift - Delete

Delete the selected item permanently without placing the item in the Recycle Bin

By default, when you delete a file or folder using Shift - Delete, Windows confirms that you want to delete it:

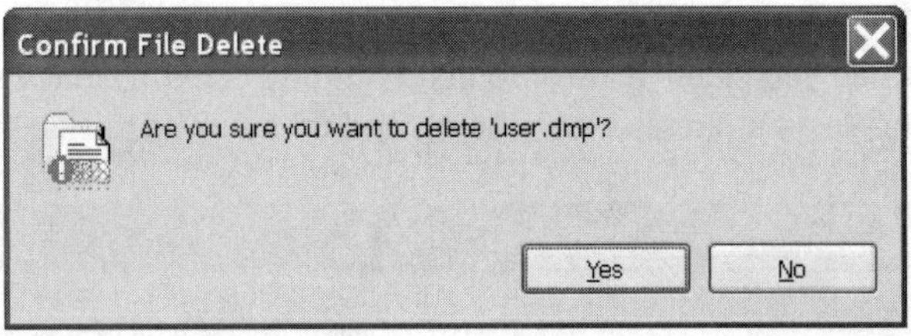

To delete files without confirmation, display the Recycle Bin Properties dialog box (shown in Figure 2-4), and then clear the Display Delete Confirmation Dialog check box on the Global tab (to affect all drives) or on the tab for the drive you want to affect.

Editing Text in a Windows Explorer Window

Once you've reached the file or folder you want to affect, you can rename it by displaying an edit box around it and typing the new name.

[F2]

Display an edit box on the selected file or folder name

[🔲 user.dmp]] Press this shortcut to display an edit box (as shown here) so that you can edit a file name or folder name. Type the new name and press [Enter] (or click elsewhere) to apply it. Press [Esc] to remove the edit box without making the change. This shortcut works both in Windows Explorer windows and in common dialog boxes.

[Ctrl]-[←]

Move the insertion point to the start of the current or previous word

If the insertion point is in a word, this shortcut moves the insertion point to the beginning of that word; if the insertion point is between words, the shortcut moves the insertion point to the beginning of the previous word. This shortcut works both in most text editors (for example, Notepad) and word processing applications (for example, WordPad and Word) but also in Windows edit boxes (for example, in a Windows Explorer window).

[Ctrl]-[→]

Move the insertion point to the start of the next word

This shortcut works both in most text editors (for example, Notepad) and word processing applications (for example, WordPad and Word) but also in Windows edit boxes (for example, in a Windows Explorer window).

[Ctrl]-[Home]

Move the insertion point to the start of the line

[Ctrl]-[End]

Move the insertion point to the end of the line

Manipulating Application Windows

Windows offers a good variety of keyboard shortcuts for manipulating application windows and switching among them. These keyboard shortcuts work for Windows Explorer windows and for almost all Windows applications.

Shortcuts for Manipulating Application Windows

Alt - F4

Exit the application or close the dialog box

This shortcut closes the active window and usually exits the application. For example, pressing this shortcut in Notepad exits Notepad. But if you have a dialog box such as the Open dialog box displayed, pressing this shortcut closes the dialog box without exiting the application.

Alt - Spacebar

Display the control menu for the active application window

The control menu (shown here) typically contains commands for moving, restoring, resizing, minimizing, maximizing, or closing the window. The control menu for a dialog box typically contains only a Move command and a Close command.

KBC IBM/R KEYBOAR

   Restore
   Move
   Size
  — Minimize
  □ Maximize
  ✕ Close   Alt+F4

Alt - -

Display the control menu for the active document window

The control menu for a document window contains commands for moving, restoring, resizing, minimizing, maximizing, or closing the window.

>> **Note:** *Usually, only one of* Alt - Spacebar *and* Alt - - *works for any given window, but with some applications, both shortcuts work. If you find that one doesn't work for a particular window, try the other.*

Ctrl - F4

Close the active document

In applications that enable you to have multiple documents open at the same time (for example, Word or Excel), this shortcut closes the active document. In applications that don't support multiple open documents (for example, Notepad), this shortcut has no effect.

F10

Activate the menu bar in the active application

Pressing F10 has the same effect as pressing Alt on its own: it puts the focus on the first menu item in the menu bar (usually the File menu).

Shortcuts for Switching Among Running Applications

Instead of switching among your running applications by using the mouse and the taskbar, you can use the following three keyboard shortcuts.

Alt-Tab

Switch forward between the open applications

Press Alt-Tab to display the "coolswitch" menu of running applications (shown here). Keep holding down Alt and press Tab to select the application you want. Then release Alt to switch to that application.

KBC 80 3000 CHERRY GOLD CROSS POINT KE...

Alt-Shift-Tab

Switch backward between the open applications

Press Alt-Shift-Tab to display the "coolswitch" menu of running applications. Keep holding down Alt and Shift and press Tab to select the application you want. Then release Alt and Shift to switch to that application.

Alt-Esc

Cycle through open applications in the order you opened them

Hold down Alt and press Esc to activate each open application in turn. Release Esc when you've activated the application you want to use.

Shortcuts for Navigating in Dialog Boxes

Windows XP supports the following keyboard shortcuts for navigating in dialog boxes.

Ctrl-Tab

Move forward through the tabs (from left to right)

When you press Ctrl-Tab, Windows XP displays the next tab.

Ctrl-Shift-Tab

Move backward through the tabs (from right to left)

[Tab]

Move forward through the controls in a dialog box

Windows XP displays a dotted outline around the control to which you've moved the focus. [Tab] treats a group of option buttons as a single control, so when you've accessed a group of option buttons, use the arrow keys to move the focus among them. Windows XP selects the option button that has the focus.

[Shift]-[Tab]

Move backward through the controls in a dialog box

Windows XP displays a dotted outline around the control to which you've moved the focus.

[Alt]-access key

Select the control associated with the access key

The effect of this shortcut depends on the control that the access key is associated with. For example:

- Pressing the access key for an option button selects that option button and clears the other option buttons in the option group.
- Pressing the access key for a check box toggles the check box between selected and cleared (in effect, reversing the current state).
- Pressing the access key for a command button (for example, the OK button) "clicks" that button.

[Enter]

"Click" the selected option or button

Pressing [Enter] "clicks" the control that currently has the focus in the dialog box.

[Spacebar]

Toggle the state of the selected check box

Pressing [Spacebar] clears a selected check box and selects a cleared check box.

[←], [→], [↑], [↓]

Move the focus among a group of option buttons

When you move the focus with an arrow key, Windows XP selects the option button that has the focus.

F1

Display Help for the current dialog box or tab, if available

F4

Display or hide the selected drop-down list

After selecting a drop-down list (for example, by pressing Tab)), press F4 to display the list. You can then press ↓ to navigate down the list. Press F4 again to hide the list once more.

Backspace

Move up to the parent folder

In the Open dialog box or the Save As dialog box, select a folder and press Backspace to move up to the parent folder.

Working with Remote Desktop Connection

Remote Desktop Connection is a remote-control technology that lets you connect to a remote computer on which you have a user account and work on that computer almost exactly as if you were sitting at it. The remote computer must be running Windows XP Professional, Windows 2000 Server, or Windows Server 2003, and must have the Remote Desktop component configured for remote access. The home computer (the one you're physically at) can be running Windows XP Home Edition or Windows XP Professional.

Remote Desktop Connection uses variations on Windows XP's standard keyboard shortcuts so that the home computer knows which commands you're giving to it and which commands you're giving to the remote computer.

Remote Desktop Connection Shortcuts

Alt-Home

Display the Start menu

This shortcut is the equivalent of pressing 🏢 or Ctrl-Esc on the local computer.

Ctrl-Alt-End

Display the Windows Task Manager window or the Windows Security dialog box

Use the Windows Task Manager window to identify performance issues on the remote computer, shut down applications, or restart Windows. The Windows

Security dialog box provides buttons for accessing Windows Task Manager, logging off, locking the computer, and shutting down the computer.

[Alt]-[Page Up]

Switch forward between the open applications on the remote computer

This shortcut is the equivalent of pressing [Alt]-[Tab] on the local computer.

[Alt]-[Page Down]

Switch backward between the open applications on the remote computer

This shortcut is the equivalent of pressing [Alt]-[Shift]-[Tab] on the local computer.

[Alt]-[Insert]

Cycle through the open applications in the order you opened them

This shortcut is the equivalent of pressing [Alt]-[Esc] on the local computer.

[Ctrl]-[Alt]-[Break]

Toggle the RDC client between a window and full screen

[Alt]-[Delete]

Display the control menu

This shortcut is the equivalent of pressing [Alt]-[Spacebar] on the local computer.

[Ctrl]-[Alt]-[-]

Capture the active window to the Clipboard

This shortcut is the equivalent of pressing [Alt]-[Print Screen] on the local computer.

[Ctrl]-[Alt]-[+]

Capture the Remote Desktop Connection window to the Clipboard

This shortcut is the equivalent of pressing [Print Screen] on the local computer.

Working with Accessibility Options

As you saw in Chapter 1, Windows XP offers several accessibility options for making the keyboard easier to use: FilterKeys, StickyKeys, ToggleKeys, and MouseKeys. Appropriately enough, you can turn these accessibility options on and off from the keyboard as well as with the mouse.

Accessibility Shortcuts

`Right Shift` for eight seconds

Toggle FilterKeys on or off

When you hold down `Right Shift` for eight seconds, Windows XP displays the
FilterKeys dialog box shown here. Click the OK button to turn FilterKeys on.

> **FilterKeys**   ☒
>
> Holding down the right SHIFT key for 8 seconds turns on FilterKeys. FilterKeys
> causes Windows to ignore brief or repeated keystrokes and slows down the
> keyboard repeat rate.
>
> To keep FilterKeys on, click OK.
> To cancel FilterKeys, click Cancel.
> To deactivate the key combination for FilterKeys, click Settings.
>
>   OK   Cancel   Settings

`Left Alt`-`Left Shift`-`Print Screen`

Toggle the High Contrast display scheme

When you press this involved shortcut, Windows XP displays the HighContrast
dialog box shown here. Click the OK button to apply the High Contrast display
scheme. Use this shortcut again to turn off the High Contrast display scheme.

> **HighContrast**   ☒
>
> Pressing the left SHIFT, left ALT, and PRINT SCREEN keys turns on High
> Contrast. High Contrast improves readability for people with visual impairments
> by applying a special system color scheme and font size.
>
> To keep High Contrast on, click OK.
> To cancel High Contrast, click Cancel.
> To deactivate the key combination for High Contrast, click Settings.
>
>   OK   Cancel   Settings

`Left Alt`-`Left Shift`-`Num Lock`

Toggle MouseKeys on or off

When you press this shortcut, Windows XP displays the MouseKeys dialog box
shown here. Click the OK button to turn MouseKeys on.

> **MouseKeys**   ☒
>
> Pressing the left ALT, left SHIFT, and NUM LOCK keys turns on MouseKeys.
> MouseKeys lets you control the mouse pointer by using the numeric keypad on
> your keyboard.
>
> To keep MouseKeys on, click OK.
> To cancel MouseKeys, click Cancel.
> To deactivate the key combination for MouseKeys, click Settings.
>
>   OK   Cancel   Settings

Windows XP & Windows Explorer

Shift five times in sequence

Toggle StickyKeys on or off

When you press Shift five times in quick succession, Windows XP displays the StickyKeys dialog box shown here. Click the OK button to turn StickyKeys on.

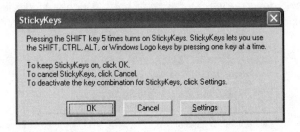

NumLock for five seconds

Toggle ToggleKeys on or off

When you hold down NumLock for five seconds, Windows XP displays the ToggleKeys dialog box shown here. Click the OK button to turn ToggleKeys on.

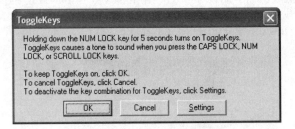

⊞-U

Open Utility Manager

3

Office's Shared Keyboard Shortcuts and AutoCorrect

This chapter explains the keyboard shortcuts that are shared among most of the Office applications. By discussing these shortcuts together for all the applications, this chapter allows you to learn the most common shortcuts more easily, without digging through the separate chapters for each application. Also covered is the keystroke-saving tool that all the Office applications share: AutoCorrect. AutoCorrect offers subtly different features in each application, but its essence is the same in each; so to save pages and effort, it is discussed here.

The following chapters, which cover the individual applications and the shortcuts they offer, mention the shared keyboard shortcuts again briefly when a shared shortcut needs further explanation or behaves differently in an application.

Shared Keyboard Shortcuts

The Office applications share many keyboard shortcuts for common tasks such as opening and saving files, moving and resizing windows, applying basic formatting, and undoing and redoing actions. This section presents these keyboard shortcuts by category. Not every keyboard shortcut is implemented in each application, and where a keyboard shortcut is implemented, the implementation sometimes varies according to the capabilities and needs of the application in question.

Shortcuts for Opening and Saving Files

Some of the first keyboard shortcuts you should learn are those for opening and saving files, actions you'll typically perform multiple times in the course of a day.

Ctrl-O, Ctrl-F12, Ctrl-Alt-F2

Display the Open dialog box

Use one of these shortcuts to display the Open dialog box so that you can open a file. For most people, Ctrl-O is the most convenient shortcut.

Ctrl-S, Shift-F12, Alt-Shift-F2

Save the active file

When you press one of these shortcuts for a file that has never been saved before, the application displays the Save As dialog box so that you can specify the file name and the folder in which to save it. After the file has a file name, pressing one of these shortcuts saves the file under its current name.

F12

Display the Save As dialog box

Use the Save As dialog box to save the active file under a different name, in a different folder, or both.

Ctrl-P, Ctrl-Shift-F12

Display the Print dialog box

In most applications, the Print dialog box offers a range of settings for printing, but you can print immediately using your current settings by pressing Enter. The illustration shows the Print dialog box from Word 2003. Most applications also let you print without seeing the Print dialog box by clicking the Print button on the Standard toolbar.

Shortcuts for Moving and Resizing Windows

To work efficiently with windows, you'll often need to resize them and rearrange them. You can manipulate windows with the mouse, but you can also manipulate them by using the following keyboard shortcuts.

Ctrl - F10

Maximize or restore the active document window

Pressing this shortcut maximizes the active document window so that it occupies the full space within the application window. To see the document at the largest size possible, maximize the application window as well. If the active document window is already maximized, pressing this shortcut restores it to its previous size.

Ctrl - F5

Restore the active document window

This shortcut is the equivalent of clicking the Restore Window button on the window's title bar.

Ctrl - F7

Move the active document window

Press this shortcut, use the arrow keys to move the window, and then press Enter to complete the move. The active document window must be "restored" rather than maximized, because you cannot move a maximized window.

Ctrl - F8

Resize the active document window

Press this shortcut, use the arrow keys to drag the window's borders to the size you want, and then press Enter to complete the resizing.

Alt - F4

Close the active window, exit the application, or both

Pressing this shortcut either closes the active window or exits the application, depending on how the application implements windows containing different files. If the window you're closing is the last open window for the active file, and the file contains unsaved changes, the application prompts you to save them.

Ctrl - F4, Ctrl - W

Close the active window

If the window you're closing is the last open window for the active file, and the file contains unsaved changes, the application prompts you to save them.

Working with Text

Windows and most applications support the following keyboard shortcuts for working with text.

Shortcuts for Deleting Text

You can use the following keyboard shortcuts for deleting text.

Backspace

Delete one character to the left of the insertion point

Ctrl - Backspace

Delete one word to the left of the insertion point

Delete

Delete one character to the right of the insertion point

Shift - Delete

Delete one word to the right of the insertion point

Shortcuts for Moving Around in Text

You can use the following keyboard shortcuts to move the insertion point around in text.

←

Move one character to the left

→

Move one character to the right

↑

Move up one line

↓

Move down one line

Ctrl - ←

Move one word to the left

Ctrl-→

> *Move one word to the right*

Home

> *Move to the beginning of the line*

End

> *Move to the end of the line*

Ctrl-↑

> *Move up one paragraph*

Ctrl-↓

> *Move down one paragraph*

Ctrl-Home

> *Move to the beginning of the current item*

The exact effect of this shortcut depends on what the current item is. For example, pressing Ctrl-Home in a text box moves the insertion point to the beginning of the text box. Pressing Ctrl-Home in a Word document moves the insertion point to the beginning of the document.

Ctrl-End

> *Move to the end of the current item*

The exact effect of this shortcut depends on what the current item is. For example, pressing Ctrl-End in a text box moves the insertion point to the end of the text box. Pressing Ctrl-End in a Word document moves the insertion point to the end of the document.

Shortcuts for Selecting Text and Objects

You can use the following keyboard shortcuts to select text and objects.

Shift-→

> *Select the next character to the right*

Shift-←

> *Select the next character to the left*

Ctrl-Shift-→

Select to the end of the current word or next word

If the insertion point is in a word, pressing Ctrl-Shift-→ selects to the end of that word. If the insertion point is between words, pressing this shortcut selects to the end of the next word.

Ctrl-Shift-←

Select to the beginning of the current word or previous word

If the insertion point is in a word, pressing Ctrl-Shift-← selects to the start of that word. If the insertion point is between words, pressing this shortcut selects to the start of the previous word.

Shift-↑

Select one line up

Shift-↓

Select one line down

Tab

Move the focus to the next object

Shift-Tab

Move the focus to the previous object

Working with Dialog Boxes

You can use the following keyboard shortcuts to work with dialog boxes in Windows.

Shortcuts for Working with Standard Dialog Boxes

Enter

Click the default button in the dialog box

Esc

Click the Cancel button

Ctrl-Tab, Ctrl-Page Down

Display the next tab of the dialog box

Ctrl-Shift-Tab, Ctrl-Page Up

Display the previous tab

Alt-F4

Close the dialog box

F4

Display a drop-down list

Shortcuts for Working in Common Dialog Boxes

You can use the following shortcuts for taking actions from the keyboard in the Open dialog box, the Save As dialog box, and the Insert Picture dialog box.

F4

Toggle the display of the Look In drop-down list

F5

Refresh the list of files

Alt-1

Display the previous folder

This shortcut is the equivalent of clicking the Back button.

Alt-2

Display the parent folder of the current folder

This shortcut is the equivalent of clicking the Up button.

Alt-3

Close the dialog box and display your web search page in the default browser

This shortcut is the equivalent of clicking the Search the Web button.

Alt-4

Delete the selected file or folder

This shortcut is the equivalent of clicking the Delete button.

Alt-5

Create a new folder in the current folder

This shortcut is the equivalent of clicking the Create New Folder button.

Shared Shortcuts and AutoCorrect

Alt-6

Cycle to the next folder view

Press this shortcut one or more times to move from List view to Details view to Properties view to Preview, and then back to List view. This shortcut is the equivalent of choosing one of the view items from the View drop-down menu.

Alt-7, Alt-L

Display the Tools drop-down menu

Applying Basic Formatting

The following shortcuts for applying basic formatting are widely used throughout the Office applications. You can also apply the formatting by clicking the appropriate button on the Formatting toolbar in most of the applications.

Shortcuts for Formatting

Ctrl-B

Toggle boldface

Ctrl-I

Toggle italic

Ctrl-U

Toggle single underline

  Single underline puts a continuous line under the selected words and spaces. Some applications offer other types of underlining, such as word underline (each word underlined, but not spaces) and double underline.

Ctrl-L

Apply left alignment

>> **Note:** *The* Ctrl-L, Ctrl-E, *and* Ctrl-R *shortcuts don't apply alignment in Excel.*

Ctrl-E

Apply centering

```
≡
```

Ctrl-R

Apply right alignment

```
≡
```

Cutting, Copying, and Pasting

The Office applications support both the standard Windows keyboard shortcuts and the older shortcuts for cutting, copying, and pasting objects. You can also cut, copy, and paste by using the buttons on the Standard toolbar in most of the applications.

Office uses not one but two Clipboards—the standard Clipboard built into Windows, which is available to all applications, and the Office Clipboard, which is available only to the Office applications. The Windows Clipboard can hold only one item at once, so each subsequent Copy or Cut command overwrites the existing contents of the Clipboard with the new item. The Office Clipboard can hold up to 24 items at the same time, enabling you to copy (or cut) a series of items to the Clipboard and then paste them one after the other in the order that suits you.

Office 2000 implements the Office Clipboard as a toolbar, while Office XP and Office 2003 implement it as a task pane. Here's the Office 2003 Clipboard with several items on it:

Shared Shortcuts and AutoCorrect

By default, the Office applications display the Office Clipboard when you perform two or more Cut or Copy operations, or a mixture of the two, without performing a Paste operation between them. You can also display the Office Clipboard manually by pressing [Ctrl]-[C] twice, choosing Edit | Office Clipboard, or by choosing its entry on the drop-down menu in the task pane.

Here's how to use the Office Clipboard:

- Scroll up and down to see items that don't fit within the display.
- To paste an item, position the insertion point where you want the item to appear, and then click the item on the Office Clipboard.
- To paste all items, position the insertion point and click Paste All.
- To clear the Office Clipboard of all its current contents, click Clear All.
- To delete an item, right-click it and choose Delete from the shortcut menu.

Once you start using the Office Clipboard, Office displays a taskbar icon in the notification area by default. The context menu for this icon contains the commands Show Office Clipboard, Clear All, and Stop Collecting. The context menu also has an Options submenu that provides quick access to the configuration options discussed next.

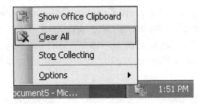

To control how the Office Clipboard behaves, click the Options button at the bottom of its task pane or the Options submenu button on the notification area icon's context menu:

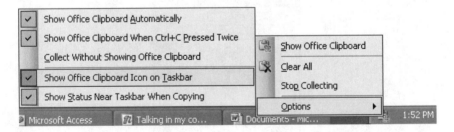

You can then toggle the following options on and off:

- **Show Office Clipboard Automatically**   Controls whether Office displays the Clipboard task pane automatically.

- **Show Office Clipboard When Ctrl+C Pressed Twice**   Controls whether Office displays the Clipboard automatically when you press [Ctrl]-[C] twice in succession. Clear this check box if you prefer to display the Office Clipboard manually.

- **Collect Without Showing Office Clipboard**   Controls whether Office displays the Clipboard automatically once you've performed two Copy or Cut operations without a Paste operation between them. Select this option if you don't want the Clipboard task pane taking up space on screen while you're making a collection of cut or copied items to paste.

- **Show Office Clipboard Icon on Taskbar**   Controls whether Office displays the Clipboard icon on the taskbar.

- **Show Status Near Taskbar When Copying**   Controls whether Office displays an informational pop-up (for example, *Item 12 of 24 Clipboard Items Collected*) over the notification area when you cut or copy an item to the Office Clipboard. If you find the status messages distracting, turn them off.

When you paste an item, Office retains as much of the formatting as possible. To change the format of an item you've pasted, click its Smart Tag and choose a different paste option from the resulting menu. A Smart Tag is an active button that appears in a document and gives you access to actions you may need to perform. Here's an example showing the paste options available after pasting a cell from an Excel worksheet into a Word document:

Office 2000 » Smart Tags aren't supported in Office 2000, but you can control the format in which you paste an item by choosing Edit | Paste Special and choosing the paste format in the Paste Special dialog box instead of simply pasting the item. You can use the Paste Special dialog box in Office XP and Office 2003 as well, but in general, using the Paste Options Smart Tag is faster and more convenient.

Shortcuts for Cut, Copy, and Paste

Ctrl-C, Ctrl-Insert

Copy the current selection to the Windows Clipboard and the Office Clipboard

Ctrl-V, Shift-Insert

Paste the current contents of the Windows Clipboard

Ctrl-X, Shift-Delete

Cut the current selection to the Windows Clipboard and the Office Clipboard

Alt-Shift-F10

Display the contents of the current or next Smart Tag

Office 2000 » The Office 2000 applications don't support Smart Tags, so this shortcut doesn't work in them.

Capturing the Screen

Windows lets you easily capture either the full screen or the active window as a graphic. The capture operation places the screen or window on the Clipboard. You can then paste it into an Office document or a graphics application.

Shortcuts for Capturing the Screen

[Print Screen]

Copy the screen to the Windows Clipboard as a picture

[Alt]-[Print Screen]

Copy the active window to the Clipboard as a picture

Pressing [Alt]-[Print Screen] copies just the active window, rather than the entire screen, to the Office Clipboard.

Getting Help

The Office applications support full-featured help, together with two shortcuts for accessing that help.

Shortcuts for Getting Help

[F1]

Launch Help

The Office 2003 applications display the Help task pane. The Office 2000 and Office XP applications by default display the Office Assistant. If you turn off the Office Assistant, Office 2000 and Office XP display the application's Help file in a separate window. (To turn off the Office Assistant, click the Options button to display the Options tab of the Office Assistant dialog box, clear the Use the Office Assistant check box, and then click the OK button.)

[Shift]-[F1]

Launch What's This? Help

What's This? Help displays a question mark next to the mouse pointer. You then click on an object in the application window to display a ScreenTip of help about that object. Press [Esc] to turn off What's This? Help. **Word 2003 »** In Word 2003, [Shift]-[F1] displays the Reveal Formatting task pane. **Excel »** Excel doesn't use the [Shift]-[F1] shortcut.

Launching the Visual Basic Editor and the Microsoft Script Editor

All the Office applications except OneNote support Visual Basic for Applications, the programming language built into Office for recording macros and writing code.

Word, Excel, PowerPoint, and Access support the Microsoft Script Editor, a tool that programmers can use to create scripts for web pages created in the Office applications.

Shortcuts for Launching the Visual Basic Editor and Script Editor

Alt - F11

Display the Visual Basic Editor

Alt - Shift - F11

Display the Microsoft Script Editor

Alt - F8

Display the Macros dialog box

From the Macros dialog box, you can run an existing macro or open a macro for editing in the Visual Basic Editor. The advantage to opening the Visual Basic Editor via the Macros dialog box rather than directly via the Alt - F11 keyboard shortcut is that you can make Visual Basic display the macro you want to edit, rather than having to navigate to it manually.

Undoing, Redoing, and Repeating Actions

The Office applications provide keyboard shortcuts for undoing actions, redoing undone actions, and repeating the last action.

Shortcuts for Undoing, Redoing, and Repeating Actions

Ctrl-Z

Undo the previous action

Most of the Office applications support multiple levels of Undo. Each Ctrl-Z keypress undoes one action, so you can undo multiple actions by issuing the shortcut multiple times.

Ctrl-Y, F4

Redo or repeat the previous action

If you've just undone an action, this shortcut redoes the action. If not, this shortcut repeats the previous action. If you're not sure which action will be redone or repeated when you issue this shortcut, display the Edit menu and check the second command, which will read "Redo Delete," "Repeat Typing," or a similar brief description. **Outlook »** The redo/repeat shortcut doesn't work in Outlook.

Finding and Replacing Items

The Office applications provide powerful Find and Replace functionality. The specific features of the Find and Replace functions vary depending on the capabilities of the application—for example, Word lets you search for styles, while Excel lets you constrain a search to a worksheet. But you can invoke the Find and Replace functions by using the same keyboard shortcuts in each of the applications.

Shortcuts for Find and Replace

Ctrl-F

Display the Find dialog box or Find tab

Ctrl-H

Display the Replace dialog box or Replace tab

Shared Shortcuts and AutoCorrect

Invoking Frequently Used Tools

The Office applications offer keyboard shortcuts for invoking frequently used tools, such as the Insert Hyperlink dialog box and the Spelling Checker.

Shortcuts for Invoking Frequently Used Tools

Ctrl - K

Display the Insert Hyperlink dialog box

The Insert Hyperlink dialog box lets you insert a hyperlink at the current selection. The options available vary depending on the application. This illustration shows the Insert Hyperlink dialog box for Word 2003:

F7

Run the Spelling Checker

The Spelling Checker scans the file or the current selection for spelling errors and displays suggested corrections for apparent errors that it finds.

The Spelling Checker for Word (and Outlook, when Outlook is using Word as its e-mail editor) incorporates a Grammar Checker, which automatically checks the grammar in the document.

Alt - click

Display information about the word in the Research task pane

The Research task pane is available only in the Office 2003 applications.

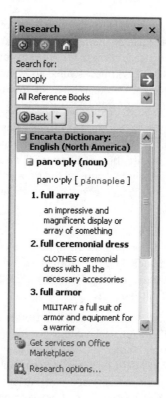

⇧ Shift ‑ F7

Look up the word in the Thesaurus dialog box

The Thesaurus is available in Word, PowerPoint, and Publisher. In Office 2003, the Thesaurus is implemented as part of the Research task pane. In Office XP and Office 2000, the Thesaurus is implemented as a dialog box.

Saving Keystrokes and Time with AutoCorrect

Office has the mother of all keyboard shortcuts built into it in the form of AutoCorrect. Most Office users fail to appreciate the extent of AutoCorrect's capabilities and so don't use it fully; but you, in your quest to become a keyboard-shortcut fiend, can be the exception. This section explains what AutoCorrect is, how it works, and how you can get the most out of it.

What AutoCorrect Is

If you've used the Office applications at all, you've probably bumped into AutoCorrect. It's the feature that watches as you type and makes corrections automatically when you type characters that match one of its entries. For example, if you type "abbout" and a space (or another character that triggers an AutoCorrect check), AutoCorrect automatically corrects the word to "about." Office ships with an impressive list of AutoCorrect entries—Office 2003 includes more than 900 entries altogether—and you can create as many of your own entries as you want.

If you've worked with older word processing applications, you may remember what were confusingly called "glossaries." A *glossary* was a block of text that you could define an abbreviation for, type the abbreviation, and then invoke the Glossary command to substitute the text block for the abbreviation. AutoCorrect is an automatic form of glossary that runs all the time and checks each group of characters you type. Word also includes manual glossaries, which are now called AutoText.

AutoCorrect is implemented in all the major Office applications, but works in somewhat different ways depending on the application. Word has the most extensive implementation, including both formatted AutoCorrect entries and unformatted (text) AutoCorrect entries. The other applications use only unformatted AutoCorrect entries.

So that each application can access them, Office stores unformatted AutoCorrect entries centrally in the MSO*nnnn*.acl file in the *%userprofile%*\Application Data\ Microsoft\Office folder. Here, *%userprofile%* is the path to your user profile (for example, C:\Documents and Settings\Randall Poe\Application Data\Microsoft\ Office), and *nnnn* is the numeric designation for the localization of Office you're using. For example, U.S. English AutoCorrect entries are stored in the MSO1033.acl file.

>> *Tip:* *if you use AutoCorrect extensively, and invest time and effort in creating custom AutoCorrect entries that suit your needs, back up your ACL file so that you can restore it if you have to reinstall Windows XP. If you use multiple computers, copy your ACL file from one computer to another so you don't need to re-create your AutoCorrect entries manually.*

Configuring AutoCorrect

To configure AutoCorrect and create and delete entries, you work in the AutoCorrect dialog box. The number of tabs in the AutoCorrect dialog box depends on the application: five tabs in Word (Figure 3-1); three tabs in Excel; two tabs in PowerPoint and Publisher; and a single tab in Access, Outlook, and OneNote.

Display the AutoCorrect dialog box as follows:

- In Word, Excel, PowerPoint, Publisher, OneNote, and Access, choose Tools | AutoCorrect Options.

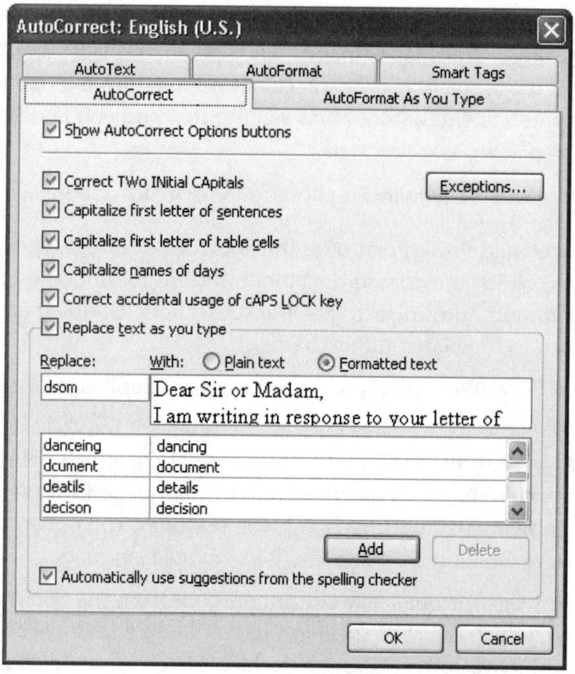

Figure 3-1   *AutoCorrect can save you many keystrokes and much effort if you use it extensively.*

Office 2000 » In Office 2000, choose Tools | AutoCorrect rather than Tools | AutoCorrect Options. The dialog box is named AutoCorrect rather than AutoCorrect Options.

- In Outlook, choose Tools | Options, click the Spelling tab, and then click AutoCorrect Options.

» Note: *By default, Outlook uses Word as its e-mail editor and inherits those of Word's AutoCorrect options that apply to Outlook as well. If you choose not to use Word as your e-mail editor, you need to select the "Use AutoCorrect When Word Isn't the E-mail Editor" option on the Spelling tab of the Options dialog box in order to use AutoCorrect.*

For each application, AutoCorrect offers five self-explanatory options for correcting two initial capitals, capitalizing the first letter of each sentence, capitalizing the names of days, correcting accidental use of CapsLock, and replacing text as you type. Setting these options is a matter of personal preference. Many people turn off the Capitalize First Letter of Sentence option because they find it annoying when they're typing notes or composing fragments of sentences.

Shared Shortcuts and AutoCorrect

AutoCorrect's most important option is Replace Text as You Type, which controls whether AutoCorrect scans for entries as you type and replaces any it finds with their designated replacement text. You'll seldom want to turn this option off, unless you're using someone else's account on a computer, and you find AutoCorrect unexpectedly replacing text you type.

AutoCorrect also offers the following application-specific options:

- Word, Excel, and PowerPoint offer the Show AutoCorrect Options Buttons check box, which provides in-document buttons for undoing corrections and configuring AutoCorrect. (See the subsection "Undoing an AutoCorrect Correction," a little later in this chapter.)

- Word and PowerPoint offer the self-explanatory Capitalize First Letter of Table Cells check box.

- Word has the Correct Keyboard Setting check box, which detects when the language you're typing is different from the language the text is configured as using and switches to the language you're typing. This option can be useful when you're working on a document in multiple languages.

- Word offers the Automatically Use Suggestions from the Spelling Checker check box, which uses the Spelling Checker as an additional correcting mechanism. AutoCorrect uses the Spelling Checker's suggestion only when AutoCorrect itself has no match and the Spelling Checker provides a single match.

Office 2000 » The Office 2000 applications don't support Smart Tags, so they don't offer the Show AutoCorrect Options Buttons check box. Word 2000 and PowerPoint 2000 don't have the Capitalize First Letter of Table Cells check box.

How AutoCorrect Works

AutoCorrect examines each character as you type. When you type a character that typically means you've finished typing a word, AutoCorrect compares the last group of characters against its list of entries. If the group of characters matches an entry, AutoCorrect substitutes the replacement text for the word. If the group of characters doesn't match an entry, AutoCorrect checks that group of characters and the previous group of characters together to see if they match an entry. If they do, AutoCorrect substitutes the replacement text. If not, AutoCorrect checks those two groups with the group before them—and so on until it has checked all the complete groups in the preceding 31 characters, at which point it gives up.

AutoCorrect entries can be up to 31 characters long and can contain spaces and punctuation. The replacement text for an entry can be up to 255 characters long—plenty to enable you to enter a short paragraph or two. (If you try to use more than 255 characters, AutoCorrect warns you that it'll need to shorten the replacement text.)

No AutoCorrect entry's name should be a real word in any language you use, because otherwise AutoCorrect will replace that word each time you try to use it. The exception is if you want to *prevent* yourself from using a particular word. For example, if the word "purchase" sends your boss into a rage, you can define AutoCorrect entries to change words based on "purchase" (purchase, purchases, purchased, purchasing, and so on) to their counterparts based on "buy." AutoCorrect will then censor your writing automatically.

AutoCorrect considers various characters to mean you've finished typing a word. These characters include spaces, punctuation, tabs, carriage returns, line feeds (Shift-Enter), and page breaks (Ctrl-Enter). Various symbols (such as % and #) also trigger AutoCorrect checks.

Creating and Deleting AutoCorrect Entries

AutoCorrect comes with a large number of built-in entries that range from simple typos (for example, "abotu" instead of "about") to basic grammatical mistakes (for example, "may of been" instead of "may have been") and some symbols (for example, AutoCorrect corrects (r) to a registered symbol, ®). You can add as many custom entries as you need. You can also replace or delete the built-in entries if you find them inconvenient.

To work with AutoCorrect entries, choose Tools | AutoCorrect Options to display the AutoCorrect dialog box. (In Outlook, choose Tools | Options, click the Spelling tab, and then click AutoCorrect Options. In Office 2000, choose Tools | AutoCorrect.)

Creating an AutoCorrect Entry

To create an AutoCorrect entry, follow these steps:

1. If the active document contains the replacement text for the AutoCorrect entry, select it. (Alternatively, copy the text from another application.)
2. Display the AutoCorrect dialog box.
3. Type the entry name in the Replace text box.
4. Type or paste the replacement text in the With text box. If you selected text in the active document in step 1, the application enters it in the With text box for you.
5. Click the Add button.

>> **Note:** *If an AutoCorrect entry with this name already exists, AutoCorrect changes the Add button to a Replace button. When you click this button, AutoCorrect prompts you to decide whether to overwrite the existing entry with the new entry.*

Deleting an AutoCorrect Entry

To delete an AutoCorrect entry, select it in the list box (scroll or type down to it) and click the Delete button.

Renaming an AutoCorrect Entry

To change the name of an existing AutoCorrect entry, select it in the list so that the application enters the entry's name in the Replace text box and its contents in the With text box. Type the new name and click the Add button to create a new entry with that name and contents. Then delete the old entry.

Creating AutoCorrect Entries from Misspelled Words in Word

In Word, you can also create AutoCorrect entries from misspelled words the Spelling Checker has identified:

- Right-click a word the Spelling Checker has flagged with its red underline, and then choose the correct word from the AutoCorrect submenu.
- From the Spelling and Grammar dialog box, select the correct word in the Suggestions list box, and then click the AutoCorrect button.

Word corrects the term in the text and adds an AutoCorrect entry for the misspelling.

Creating Formatted AutoCorrect Entries in Word

In Word (and in Outlook, when you're using Word as the e-mail editor), you can also create formatted AutoCorrect entries. These can be text entries that contain formatting, entries that consist of graphics, or both. For example, you could create a formatted AutoCorrect entry that included your company name, address, and logo.

>> **Note:** *Word stores formatted AutoCorrect entries in your Normal template (Normal.dot). Avoid creating large numbers of graphical AutoCorrect entries, because doing so can bloat the Normal template and make it slow to load.*

To create a formatted AutoCorrect entry:

1. Enter the text and any graphics in a document, and apply formatting as needed.
2. Select the formatted items and choose Tools | AutoCorrect Options to display the AutoCorrect Options dialog box.
3. Make sure the Formatted Text option button in the Replace Text as You Type section of the AutoCorrect tab is selected. For a graphic, Word selects this option automatically. For formatted text that doesn't include a paragraph mark, you sometimes need to select it yourself.

4. Type the name for the entry. Don't duplicate the name for an unformatted entry—that's a recipe for confusion.

5. Click the Add button.

Undoing an AutoCorrect Correction

When AutoCorrect makes a correction that you don't want to keep, you can undo it by issuing an Undo command. (For example, press [Ctrl]-[Z] or click the Undo button.) But if you were typing fast at the time AutoCorrect made the change, you might need to undo a lot of typing (or other editing) before you can undo the AutoCorrect action.

To make corrections easier, Word, PowerPoint, Excel, and Outlook track corrections applied by AutoCorrect. When you hover your mouse pointer over an AutoCorrect correction, the application displays an AutoCorrect Options button that you can click to display a menu of AutoCorrect options. The options vary depending on the AutoCorrect action performed: typical choices are to undo this instance of the correction, to stop auto-capitalizing the first letter of sentences, to stop correcting this AutoCorrect entry (for the future), and to display the AutoCorrect dialog box (Control AutoCorrect Options) so you can adjust other options.

Office 2000 » The Office 2000 applications don't support Smart Tags, so they don't let you undo AutoCorrect corrections in this way.

Using AutoCorrect Effectively to Save Yourself Keystrokes

Here are three suggestions for making the most of AutoCorrect:

- **Define longer AutoCorrect entries**   AutoCorrect is wonderful for fixing typos as you type. But if you work extensively with text, consider using AutoCorrect to accelerate your typing by defining AutoCorrect entries for long words, phrases, sentences, or even paragraphs you use frequently. As mentioned earlier, the limit for an AutoCorrect entry is 255 characters, but you can use several entries in sequence. (You can also use AutoText entries instead. See the next chapter.)

- **Use AutoCorrect for enforcing consistency**   Because AutoCorrect can change up to the last 31 characters, you can create AutoCorrect entries to correct whole phrases that you (or other people) get wrong. For example, if your company changes the name of its Quality Control Department to Quality Assurance Department, you might create an AutoCorrect entry to change "Quality Control Department" to "Quality Assurance Department" to help ensure the change was made throughout all documents you subsequently created. (You should probably also create a shorter AutoCorrect entry for the department's name.)

Shared Shortcuts and AutoCorrect

- **Create multiple AutoCorrect entries to fix the same problem**   If you create many AutoCorrect entries, remembering entries you use less frequently may be a problem. But there's nothing to stop you from creating multiple entries for the same replacement text. You can also create multiple AutoCorrect entries to fix assorted misspellings of common words. For example, you might create AutoCorrect entries to change typos such as *thoug, thogh, thouh,* and other variations to "though."

Adding and Deleting AutoCorrect Exceptions

Once you get the hang of AutoCorrect, you'll find it an invaluable weapon in your battle against wasted keystrokes. But sometimes you'll find that AutoCorrect corrects a term you don't want it to correct. When this happens, you can prevent AutoCorrect from repeating the mistake by defining an AutoCorrect exception. To do so, click the Exceptions button on the AutoCorrect tab of the AutoCorrect Options dialog box and use the controls in the AutoCorrect Exceptions dialog box:

All the Office applications provide first-letter exceptions (for abbreviations such as corp. and for similar terms that end with punctuation) and initial-caps exceptions (for example, IDs). Word also provides "other exceptions," which let you define exceptions that fall outside those categories.

4

Word Keyboard Shortcuts

Of all the Office applications, Word is perhaps the best suited to using keyboard shortcuts. First, a typical Word document has more text and fewer graphical objects than a typical document in any other Office application (with the possible exception of an Outlook e-mail message), so it's convenient to work with the keyboard. Second, Word comes with many built-in keyboard shortcuts that cover a wide variety of actions. Third, Microsoft has made Word very easy to customize, so you can create new keyboard shortcuts and change the built-in keyboard shortcuts as needed.

We'll start with Word's built-in shortcuts and then move on to customizing keyboard shortcuts.

Word's Built-in Shortcuts

Word has more shortcuts than most of the other Office applications put together. This section presents them broken into subsections by topic. We'll start with the differences worth noting about Word's implementation of the shared Office keyboard shortcuts.

Notes on the Shared Office Keyboard Shortcuts

Word uses the standard Office keyboard shortcuts discussed in "Shared Keyboard Shortcuts" in Chapter 3. The following keyboard shortcuts have differences worth noting.

Shortcuts for Moving and Resizing Windows

In addition to the standard keyboard shortcuts discussed in Chapter 3, Word supports two other keyboard shortcuts.

Alt - F10

Maximize the application window

Alt - F5

Restore the application window

Shortcuts for Creating and Saving Documents

Word's keyboard shortcuts for creating and saving documents are standard except for the Ctrl-N keyboard shortcut.

Ctrl - N

Create a new document using the default template

The default template is named Normal.dot and is loaded automatically when you launch Word. Normal.dot contains the default settings for Word documents—for example, the default font.

Shortcuts for Revealing Formatting

Word uses the Shift-F1 shortcut to display formatting information about the selection.

Shift - F1

Launch What's This? Help or display the Reveal Formatting task pane

When you press Shift-F1, Word 2003 displays the Reveal Formatting task pane, which displays information on font, paragraph, and section formatting. Word XP displays the What's This? Help question-mark pointer; if you click a document object, Word displays the Reveal Formatting task pane, shown in the following illustration.

Word 2000 » Word 2000 doesn't have task panes; when you press Shift-F1, Word 2000 displays the What's This? Help pointer. If you click a document object, Word 2000 displays a ScreenTip with information about the object's formatting.

```
Reveal Formatting                    ▼ ✕
 ⊕ | ⊕ | ⌂
Selected text

  aid

  ☐ Compare to another selection
Formatting of selected text
 ⊟ Font
 Font:
   (Default) Arial
   10 pt
 Language:
   English (U.S.)

 ⊞ Paragraph
 ⊟ Section
 Margins:
   Left:  1.25"
   Right: 1.25"
   Top:   1"
   Bottom: 1"
Options
  ☐ Distinguish style source
  ☐ Show all formatting marks
```

Changing the View

Word's many views—including Normal view, Outline view, Print Layout view, Web Layout view, and Print Preview—enable you to see exactly the parts of the document that you need to work with. Word lets you change the view easily from the keyboard or using the mouse.

Shortcuts for Changing the View

[Ctrl]-[Alt]-[N]

Apply Normal view

Normal view tends to be the best view for composing and editing text without worrying about its layout. You can also apply Normal view by choosing View | Normal or clicking the Normal button on the horizontal scroll bar.

Word 2003

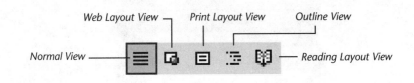

Web Layout View ─┐   Print Layout View   Outline View

Normal View ────────   ──── Reading Layout View

Ctrl - Alt - O

Apply Outline view

Pressing this keyboard shortcut displays the active document in Outline view with the level of headings shown that you were last using in Outline view in this Word session. If this is the first time you've used Outline view in this Word session, you will probably need to explicitly specify the level of headings you want Word to display.

You can also apply Outline view by choosing View | Outline or clicking the Outline button on the horizontal scroll bar.

Alt - Shift - 1 to 9

Display Outline Level 1–9

Press Alt - Shift and the appropriate number for the number of heading levels you want to display. For example, press Alt - Shift - 1 to display Outline Level 1 paragraphs only, Alt - Shift - 2 to display up to Outline Level 2 paragraphs, and Alt - Shift - 9 to display up to Outline Level 9 paragraphs.

Ctrl - Alt - P

Apply Print Layout view

Print Layout view displays the active document approximately as it will print with the current printer. Print Layout view is similar to Print Preview but provides fuller editing capabilities. In Print Layout view, you can see where the headers and footers will appear, where the margins will fall, and where each line will break.

You can also apply Print Layout view by choosing View | Print Layout or clicking the Print Layout button on the horizontal scroll bar.

Ctrl - F2, Ctrl - Alt - I

Toggle Print Preview

Print Preview displays the active document as it will print with the current printer. Print Preview provides tools for working with the margins and the page setup of the document. You can also switch to Print Preview by clicking the Print Preview button on the Standard toolbar.

While Print Preview is primarily designed for making sure your documents look right before you print hard copies of them (or fax them from your PC), you can also use Print Preview for editing your documents. This capability is especially useful if your monitor is large enough to display two pages at once side by side, because you can see how the changes you make on the current page affect the next page.

 By default, Word switches to Magnifier mode when you display a document in Print Preview. To switch to Edit mode, click the Magnifier button.

Ctrl-* on the number row

Toggle the display of all nonprinting characters

Pressing this shortcut is the equivalent of selecting or clearing the All check box in the Formatting Marks section of the View tab of the Options dialog box (Tools | Options). Nonprinting characters include spaces, tabs, paragraph marks, optional hyphens, and hidden text.

Alt-Shift-C

Close the active pane or remove the document window split

This shortcut is particularly useful for closing the header and footer area after working in it. **Word 2003 »** In Word 2003, Alt-Shift-C removes a document slip.

Ctrl-Alt-S

Toggle horizontal splitting on the active window

Split the window horizontally into two panes when you need to view two different areas of the same document simultaneously. (Alternatively, open a new window on the document.) You can use a different view in each pane if necessary. For example, you could use Normal view for editing in one pane and Outline view for outlining in the other pane.

You can use the next set of keyboard shortcuts to move from one pane to another.

To remove the split, press Ctrl-Alt-S again.

F6, Shift-F6

Switch pane

Use these shortcuts to switch from one pane of the active document window to the next pane or the previous pane. These shortcuts work both when you've

Word 2003

split the window manually and when you're working in a view that automatically displays another pane—for example, when you have the Reviewing pane open in Normal view in Word 2003.

Ctrl-F6, Alt-F6

Activate the next document window

Use whichever of these shortcuts you find most comfortable. Because these are redundant, you might choose to reassign one of the shortcuts to another window-related command that you find useful.

Ctrl-Shift-F6, Alt-Shift-F6

Activate the previous document window

As with the next-window shortcuts, use whichever of these triple-key shortcuts you find most comfortable. (If you have only two windows open, you can use the next-window shortcuts to toggle between them—whichever window the focus is currently in, the other window is next.) Again, you might choose to reassign whichever of these shortcuts you don't use to another window-related command.

Navigating Through Documents

If you work with documents that are more than a few pages long, navigating to the appropriate points in them can become a vital part of your work. Word provides several tools and shortcuts for navigating through documents.

Shortcuts for Navigating Through Documents

Ctrl-F

Display the Find tab of the Find and Replace dialog box

Word's Find feature on the Find tab of the Find and Replace dialog box (Figure 4-1) offers a wide variety of options. You can search simply for text; or for text with specific formatting (which you specify by using the Format drop-down menu); or for formatting without text (for example, you might search for the next instance of a specific style). You can constrain the search to match case or to find only whole words rather than matches inside other words. Word XP and Word 2003 also enable you to highlight all the instances of the search term in the main document or another part of the document.

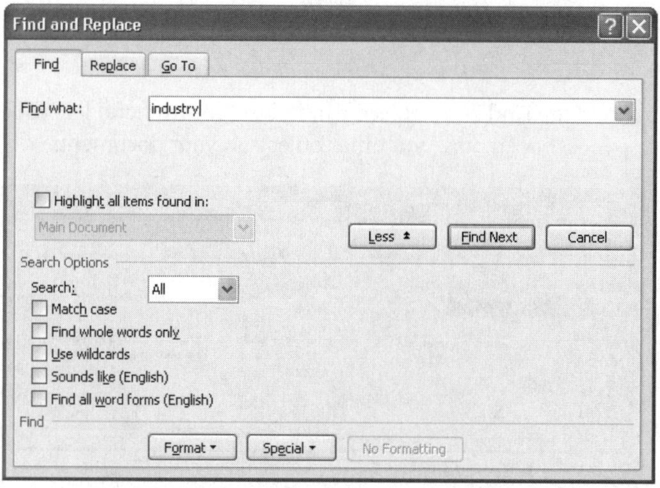

Figure 4-1 *Word's Find feature provides a wide range of options for searching for text, formatting, and special characters.*

Ctrl-H

Display the Replace tab of the Find and Replace dialog box

Word's Replace feature offers similar functions to the Find feature: you can replace text, text with specific formatting, or just formatting. Use the Find Next button to find the next instance of the search item, and the Replace button to replace the current instance. Use the Replace All button to replace all instances of the search term within the selection (if there is one) or within the active document.

Shift-F4, Ctrl-Alt-Y

Find the next occurrence of the search item

These shortcuts enable you to repeat your last search without displaying the Find and Replace dialog box. Alternatively, you can click the Next Find/Go To button at the bottom of the vertical scroll bar. The disadvantage to using the Next Find/ Go To button is that Word may be set to browse to a different browse object than Find.

>> **Note:** *Normally, you'd use the* Shift-F4 *and* Ctrl-Alt-Y *keyboard shortcuts after closing the Find and Replace dialog box. But if you choose, you can use these shortcuts with the Find and Replace dialog box still open, as long as the focus is in the document rather than in the Find and Replace dialog box.*

Word 2003

Ctrl-G, F5

Display the Go To tab of the Find and Replace dialog box

The Go To tab of the Find and Replace dialog box (shown here) lets you quickly navigate to pages, bookmarks, and other objects in your documents.

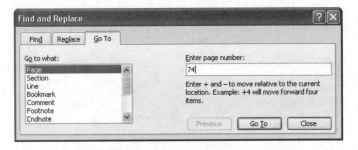

You can also display the Go To tab by double-clicking an area in the status bar that doesn't contain another control.

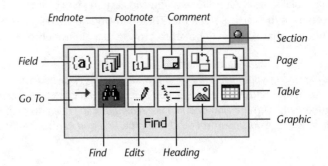

Double-click in this area to display the Go To tab
of the Find and Replace dialog box.

Ctrl-Page Down

Select the next Browse object

Use the Select Browse Object button and panel shown here to choose which object the Browse buttons control: Field, Endnote, Footnote, Comment, Section, Page, Go To, Find, Edits, Heading, Graphic, Table. For example, if you select Table in the Browse panel, you can use the Browse controls and keyboard shortcuts to navigate quickly among the tables in the document.

Performing a Find or Replace operation automatically sets the Browse object to Find. So after you've used Find and Replace, you can use (Ctrl)-(Page Up) and (Ctrl)-(Page Down) to repeat the Find operation until you change the Browse object. But because you may need to set the Browse object manually, you may find the (Shift)-(F4) and (Ctrl)-(Alt)-(Y) shortcuts more convenient for accessing the next Find item.

(Ctrl)-(Page Up)

Select the previous Browse object

When the Browse object is set to Find, this shortcut is particularly useful for finding the previous instance of the current search term.

(Ctrl)-(Shift)-(F5)

Display the Bookmark dialog box

Use bookmarks to assign names to sections of your documents so that you can access them easily either manually or when programming with VBA.

Editing Text

If you work with documents at all, you can benefit from the editing shortcuts that Word offers. These range from quickly returning to one of the last three edits made in the document to using the Spike feature for collecting a series of items cut from a document.

Shortcuts for Editing Text

(Shift)-(F5), (Ctrl)-(Alt)-(Z)

Return to the previous editing point

Word tracks the locations of the last three edits you made to a document. You can return to the last edit by pressing these shortcuts once, the second-last edit by pressing them twice, or the third-last edit by pressing them three times. Pressing a fourth time returns you to the current edit.

> **>> Note:** *What Word counts as an "edit" depends not only on the actions you take (for example, typing text or deleting text) but also the on speed at which you take the actions and the intervals between them. So using the (Shift)-(F5) and (Ctrl)-(Alt)-(Z) shortcuts may not return the insertion point to where you expect. But it's almost always worth trying before other means of navigating to other areas of the document.*

Ctrl-Y, F4, Alt-Enter

Repeat the previous action

These shortcuts all do the same thing: make Word repeat the previous editing action—for example, applying a style, typing a word or phrase, or inserting an object such as a table. If the editing action isn't what you expected, press Ctrl-Z to undo the action immediately.

Ctrl-Z, Alt-Backspace

Undo the previous action

Ctrl-Z is perhaps the most used keyboard shortcut for Windows applications. In Word, Alt-Backspace performs the same function and is more comfortable for some users.

>> **Caution:** *The previous action may not be exactly what you think. For example, if you type several words, backspace over a couple of words, and then type a correction, Word registers a single action that consists of typing those words you typed but didn't backspace over. But if you perform the same actions with pauses in between, Word usually considers typing the final words (after the backspacing) to be a separate action.*

Ctrl-A, Ctrl-5 on the numeric keypad

Select all

A Select All command selects all the contents of the current object—for example, a document or a text box. If a Select All command selects the wrong object, select the right object and issue the command again.

Ctrl-F3

Cut the selection and add it to the Spike

The Spike is a special AutoText entry to which you can cut a series of selections and then assemble them in order. You then paste the contents of the Spike into the destination. Because the Spike is destructive to the documents you're working in (you can only cut to the Spike; you can't copy to it), few people use it. The best way to use the Spike is to work on a copy of your source document or to save it, cut the material to the Spike, and then close the document without saving changes.

`Ctrl`-`Shift`-`F3`

Insert the contents of the Spike

Use this command after assembling content on the Spike as described in the previous shortcut. Inserting the contents of the Spike into a document clears the Spike.

Formatting Text

Word offers many shortcuts for applying formatting to the text in your documents.

Shortcuts for Formatting Text

`Ctrl`-`Shift`-`A`

Toggle all caps

All caps capitalizes all letters in the selection but has no effect on non-letter keys (for example, numbers)—unlike pressing `Shift` or applying `Caps Lock` and typing.

`Ctrl`-`Shift`-`K`

Toggle small caps

Small caps applies SMALL CAPITALS to all letters in the selection.

`Shift`-`F3`

Cycle the case of the selection

This shortcut cycles the case among lowercase, title case (the first letter of each word is capitalized), and uppercase (all letters are capitalized). This shortcut is an alternative to the Format | Change Case command, but that command also offers a Sentence Case option (the first letter of each sentence is capitalized) and a tOGGLE cASE command (Word inverts the capitalization of each letter).

Word 2003

Ctrl-B, Ctrl-Shift-B

Toggle boldface

Both these shortcuts work the same way, but there's no reason to use the Ctrl-Shift-B shortcut unless you've reassigned the Ctrl-B shortcut. The Ctrl-Shift-B shortcut is there for backward compatibility with older versions of Word.

Ctrl-U, Ctrl-Shift-U

Toggle underline

Both these shortcuts work the same way, but there's no reason to use the Ctrl-Shift-U shortcut (which is there for backward compatibility) unless you've reassigned the Ctrl-U shortcut.

Ctrl-Shift-W

Toggle word underline

Word underline applies an underscore to each word and to punctuation, but not to the spaces between words. Unlike the previous two shortcuts, you must press Ctrl-Shift-W to apply word underline from the keyboard; Ctrl-W is the shortcut for closing the active window.

Ctrl-Shift-D

Toggle double underlining on the selection

Ctrl-=

Toggle subscript

Subscript decreases the font size of the selected text and lowers it below the base line of the other characters.

>> **Note:** *The Character Spacing tab of the Font dialog box gives you finer control over subscripts and superscripts.*

Ctrl-+

Toggle superscript

Superscript decreases the font size of the selected text and raises it above the base line of the other characters.

Alt-X

Toggle character and character code

The character code is the Unicode number used to identify the character. Place the insertion point after the character or character code you want to toggle, and then press (Alt)-(X) to toggle it. For example, type **20AC** and then press (Alt)-(X) to toggle it to a euro symbol (€). **Word 2000 »** Word 2000 doesn't support the (Alt)-(X) keyboard shortcut.

(Ctrl)-(D)

Display the Font dialog box

If your hands are on the keyboard, this is the easiest way of displaying the Font dialog box.

(Ctrl)-(Shift)-(P)

Select the Font Size drop-down list

Use this shortcut to quickly activate the Font Size drop-down list without taking your hands off the keyboard. See also the next four shortcuts for even quicker ways of changing the font size using the keyboard.

(Ctrl)-(>)

Increase the font size in jumps

With this shortcut and the (Ctrl)-(<) shortcut, Word uses the font sizes listed in the Font Size drop-down list and the Font dialog box: 8, 9, 10, 11, 12, 14, 16, 18, and so on.

(Ctrl)-(<)

Decrease the font size in jumps

Use this shortcut to quickly decrease the font size to the next size that Word lists.

(Ctrl)-(])

Increase the font size by one point

Use this shortcut to increase the font size gradually. If you hold down this shortcut, you can wait as Word gradually increases the font size to the size you need.

(Ctrl)-([)

Decrease the font size by one point

Use this shortcut to decrease the font size gradually rather than in jumps. Again, you can hold down this shortcut and wait as Word gradually decreases the font size.

Word 2003

Ctrl-Shift-Q

Apply the Symbol font

When you need the Symbol font, this shortcut is much quicker than applying it via the Font drop-down list or the Font dialog box.

Ctrl-Shift-S

Display the Style dialog box

In Word 2000 and Word 2003, this shortcut is the quickest way of displaying the Style dialog box. **Word XP »** In Word XP, pressing Ctrl-Shift-S activates the Style drop-down list rather than displaying the Style dialog box.

Ctrl-Alt-K

AutoFormat the document

The AutoFormat operation uses the settings you've chosen on the AutoFormat tab of the AutoCorrect Options dialog box (Tools | AutoCorrect). Word displays the AutoFormat dialog box before performing the AutoFormat, so you can cancel the operation if you invoked it by mistake.

Ctrl-Shift-H

Make the selection hidden text

You can display hidden text by pressing Ctrl-Shift-* (on the number row), by selecting the All check box on the View tab of the Options dialog box (Tools | Options), or by clicking the Show/Hide ¶ button on the Standard toolbar.

Ctrl-Shift-C

Copy the formatting of the selection

 Pressing this keyboard shortcut is the equivalent of clicking the Format Painter button on the Standard toolbar: it copies the formatting of the selected text or other object to the Clipboard, so that you can paste it to other text (or another object).

Ctrl-Shift-V

Apply the copied formatting to the selection

After copying formatting using Ctrl-Shift-C (or by clicking the Format Painter button), apply the formatting to its destination by using this shortcut or by clicking the Format Painter button.

Formatting Paragraphs

The key to laying out your documents successfully in Word is to apply the correct paragraph formatting:

1. The paragraph style defines the overall formatting for the paragraph—everything from the font, font size, and font style to the line spacing and any indentation used.

2. After applying the style, you can apply any direct paragraph formatting needed to modify the style formatting just for this paragraph. For example, you might add more space before or after a particular paragraph.

3. You can then apply any character style needed for consistent character formatting of individual words or characters in the paragraph. For example, you might use a Bold Italic character style to pick out words or phrases that need extra emphasis, or apply a Superscript character style to characters that consistently need to be positioned on a higher baseline than other characters.

4. Finally, you can apply any direct character formatting needed to adjust the appearance of individual words or characters in ways that your character styles don't cover. For example, you might need to increase the font size of some characters to make them stand out, but not so many characters to make it worth creating a separate character style.

Shortcuts for Formatting Paragraphs

Word offers a good number of shortcuts for formatting paragraphs.

Ctrl-Alt-1 to 3

Apply the specified heading level to the selection

Ctrl-Alt-1 applies Heading 1 level, Ctrl-Alt-2 applies Heading 2 level, and Ctrl-Alt-3 applies Heading 3 level. Note that these shortcuts apply heading levels rather than styles: the paragraphs affected retain their current style, but take on the heading level. (You can set the outline level by using the Outline Level drop-down list on the Indents and Spacing tab of the Paragraph dialog box.)

Ctrl-Shift-L

Apply the List Bullet style to the selection

Ctrl-Shift-N, Alt-Shift-5 on the numeric keypad with Num Lock off

Apply the Normal style

Word uses the Normal style for all paragraphs that you don't explicitly apply another style to. For example, if you create a new blank document (which is based on the Normal.dot global template), you'll probably find that Word starts you off with the Normal style. When you create your own templates, set the starting paragraph to the appropriate style rather than leaving it in Normal style.

Ctrl - T

Apply or increase the hanging indent

Press this shortcut once to apply the hanging indent. Press it again to increase the hanging indent by one tab stop.

> **》 Note:** *The four indentation shortcuts discussed here don't work if you've turned off Word's AutoFormat indentation features. In Word 2003 and Word XP, these features are controlled by the "Set Left- and First-Indent with Tabs and Backspaces" check box on the AutoFormat As You Type tab of the AutoCorrect dialog box (Tools | AutoCorrect Options). In Word 2000, these features are controlled by the Tabs and Backspace Set Left Indent check box on the Edit tab of the Options dialog box (Tools | Options).*

Ctrl - Shift - T

Decrease or remove the hanging indent

Press this shortcut once to decrease the hanging indent by one tab. When the indent is hanging by a single tab, press this shortcut to remove the indent.

Ctrl - M

Increase the left indent

Each press of this shortcut increases the left indent by a single tab.

Ctrl - Shift - M

Decrease the left indent

Each press of this shortcut decreases the left indent by a single tab.

Ctrl - Q

Apply the default paragraph format of the current style

Use this shortcut to remove extra formatting that you've applied to a paragraph. For example, if you've applied direct formatting (such as bold or italic) or character styles, use this shortcut to remove them quickly and restore the paragraph's formatting to that of its paragraph style.

Ctrl-Spacebar, Ctrl-Shift-Z

Reset the formatting of the current paragraph or selection

Use this shortcut to quickly remove direct formatting that you've applied to text.

Ctrl-J

Apply justified alignment to the paragraph

Applying justified alignment to (or "justifying") a paragraph aligns the left end of its lines with the left margin and the right end of its lines with the right margin. The last line isn't aligned with the right margin unless it happens to reach the margin anyway.

Ctrl-Shift-J

Distribute the paragraph

"Distributing" a paragraph justifies all its lines, including the last line. This tends to make the last line loosely spaced but can be useful for special text effects. For more normal justification, use the standard shortcut Ctrl-J.

Ctrl-0

Add or remove extra spacing on selected paragraphs

If the selected paragraphs have no extra space, press this shortcut to add 12 points. If the selected paragraphs do have extra space, press this shortcut to remove the space.

Ctrl-1

Apply single line spacing

This shortcut (and the next two shortcuts) are useful for quickly changing the line spacing of the active paragraph or the selected paragraphs. But if you find yourself using them frequently, you should probably change the line spacing in the styles you're using.

Ctrl-5

Apply 1.5 line spacing

Ctrl-2

Apply double line spacing

Word 2003

Working with Fields

Fields can be one of the most confusing parts of a Word document. A *field* is a code that represents information stored somewhere else—either somewhere else in the same document (for example, a field that returns the contents of a bookmark), on your computer, or on a networked computer—or generated automatically (for example, a field that returns the date or the number of pages in the document).

When you insert a field in a document, Word typically displays the *field result* (the information the field returns) rather than the *field code* (text that details the information the field references). For example, the date field code **{DATE \a "dddd, MMMM dd, yyyy" *MERGEFORMAT}** might display the field result **Thursday, April 01, 2004**. You can toggle a field between displaying the field result and the field code.

To make sure a document contains the latest information available, you need to update the fields it contains. In other cases, you'll need to lock the fields in a document to prevent them from changing. When you want to freeze the current information in the fields and prevent it from changing again (even if its source is updated), you can unlink the fields from their sources.

Shortcuts for Working with Fields

[Alt]-[Shift]-[P]

Insert a page-number field at the insertion point

This shortcut is faster in most cases than using the Field dialog box (Insert | Field) to insert the page number. However, if you're working in the header and footer areas, you may find it easier to click the Insert Page Number button on the Header and Footer toolbar. The Header and Footer toolbar also includes the Insert Number of Pages button, which lets you easily create "Page 1 of 10"–style numbering.

Insert Page Number ——┘   └—— Insert Number of Pages

[Alt]-[Shift]-[D]

Insert a date field in the default format at the insertion point

The default date format depends on your Windows settings.

[Alt]-[Shift]-[T]

Insert a time field in the default format at the insertion point

The default time format depends on your Windows settings.

[Alt]-[F9]

Toggle between field codes and field results

This shortcut is the quickest way to toggle the display of field codes in the active document. You can also toggle the display of field codes by choosing Tools | Options, selecting or clearing the Field Codes check box in the Show area of the View tab of the Options dialog box, and then clicking the OK button.

[Ctrl]-[3], [Ctrl]-[F11]

Lock the fields in the current selection

Fields that you lock can't be changed until you unlock them.

[Ctrl]-[4], [Ctrl]-[Shift]-[F11]

Unlock the fields in the current selection

Unlock locked fields when you need to be able to update them again.

[F9], [Alt]-[Shift]-[U]

Update the fields in the selection

To update all the fields in a document, press [Ctrl]-[A] to select it all, and then press this shortcut.

[Ctrl]-[6], [Ctrl]-[Shift]-[F9]

Unlink the fields in the current selection

Select the fields you want to unlink before pressing either of these shortcuts. To unlink all the fields in the active document, press [Ctrl]-[A] to select all the document, and then press one of these shortcuts.

[Ctrl]-[Shift]-[F7]

Copy the modifications in a linked object back to its source file

This shortcut works only for fields that contain objects derived from, and still linked to, sources in other files.

Word 2003

Working with Outlines

Word's Outline view is a powerful tool for creating, organizing, and editing long or complex documents. Most users use the mouse extensively when working in Outline view, but if you're creating an outline, using the keyboard tends to be much faster.

Shortcuts for Working with Outlines

Ctrl-Alt-O

Apply Outline view

Alt-Shift-1 to Alt-Shift-9

Display Outline Level 1–9

Press Alt-Shift and the appropriate number for the number of heading levels you want to display. For example, press Alt-Shift-1 to display Outline Level 1 paragraphs only, Alt-Shift-2 to display up to Outline Level 2 paragraphs, and Alt-Shift-9 to display up to Outline Level 9 paragraphs.

Alt-_, Alt-Shift--

Collapse the lowest subtext in the selection

On a typical keyboard, these shortcuts are the same, because the underscore is the shifted version of the hyphen key. Select the heading you want to affect, hold down Alt-Shift, and press the hyphen key repeatedly to collapse each lowest level of the selection in turn.

Alt-+, Alt-Shift-+ on the numeric keypad

Expand the next level of subtext in the selection

Select the heading you want to affect, hold down Alt-Shift, and press the plus key once for each outline level you want to expand.

Alt-Shift-↓

Move the selection down one item in the outline

Select one or more contiguous items, and then press this shortcut to move the selection down one displayed item at a time. (For example, if you have expanded the section of the outline you're working in to show Level 3 items, each press of this shortcut moves the selection down one Level 3 item, one Level 2 item, or one Level 1 item—whichever is next in the displayed outline.)

This shortcut and the next tend to be much easier than dragging items with the mouse because they remove the chance of your changing the outline level of the item at the same time by dragging it to the left or the right.

[Alt]-[Shift]-[↑]

Move the selection up one item in the outline

Select one or more contiguous items, and then press this shortcut to move the selection up one displayed item at a time. (See the previous description for more details.)

[Alt]-[Shift]-[L]

Toggle the outline between displaying the first line of each paragraph and the full text of each paragraph

 This shortcut is the equivalent of clicking the Show First Line Only button on the Outlining toolbar.

[Alt]-[Shift]-[A]

Toggle the display of all headings and body text

This shortcut is the equivalent of selecting the Show All Levels item in the Show Level drop-down list (in Word 2003 and Word XP) or clicking the Show All Headings button on the Outlining toolbar in Word 2003.

[Alt]-[Shift]-[←], [Shift]-[Tab]

Promote the selection by one heading level

 These shortcuts are the equivalent of clicking the Promote button.

[Alt]-[Shift]-[→], [Tab]

Demote the selection by one heading level

 These shortcuts are the equivalent of clicking the Demote button.

Inserting Items

Word offers keyboard shortcuts for inserting various different items, ranging from AutoText entries to time fields, into your documents.

Shortcuts for Inserting Items

F3, Ctrl-Alt-V

Insert an AutoText entry

These shortcuts manually expand an AutoText entry into its replacement text. See "Using AutoText," at the end of this chapter, for a discussion of what AutoText is, what you can do with it, and how to do it.

Ctrl-Enter

Insert a page break at the insertion point

Inserting a page break makes Word start a new page. This method of inserting a page break is much faster than the menu method, which involves choosing Insert | Break, selecting the Page Break option button (the default) in the Break dialog box, and then clicking the OK button.

Ctrl-Shift-Enter

Insert a column break at the insertion point

Inserting a column break makes Word start a new column. You can also start a column break by choosing Insert | Break, selecting the Column Break option button in the Break dialog box, and then clicking the OK button.

Ctrl-Alt-M

Insert a comment at the insertion point

In Normal view, Word displays the Revisions pane if it's not already displayed.

Ctrl-Alt-D

Insert an endnote at the insertion point

In Normal view, Word displays the Endnotes pane if it's not already displayed.

Ctrl-Alt-F

Insert a footnote at the insertion point

In Normal view, Word displays the Footnotes pane if it's not already displayed.

Checking Your Documents

Word includes the following shortcuts for accessing its tools for checking the text of your documents and tracking changes to them.

Shortcuts for Checking Your Documents

F7

Run the Spelling and Grammar Checker

Word's default settings are to check grammar in your documents while checking the spelling. Provided that the dictionary spellings are correct, spelling is eminently suitable for checking by computer, because any particular word is spelled either correctly or incorrectly; but grammar is much less suited to checking by computer, because it is complex and full of subtleties. So while you will probably benefit from using the Spelling Checker, you may well want to turn off the Grammar Checker. To do so, choose Tools | Options, click the Spelling & Grammar tab of the Options dialog box, clear the Check Grammar with Spelling check box and the Check Grammar As You Type check box, and then click the OK button.

Alt-F7

Find the next spelling error

This shortcut is great for quickly moving from one apparent spelling error to the next in a document.

Ctrl-Shift-E

Toggle Track Changes on and off

This shortcut is an alternative to double-clicking the TRK indicator in the status bar to toggle the Track Changes setting.

| Page 1 | Sec 1 | 1/1 | At 2.3" | Ln 8 | Col 1 | REC | TRK | EXT | OVR | English (U.S | |

Ctrl-Shift-R

Update the document's word-count statistics

Word normally keeps the word-count statistics up-to-date, so you shouldn't need to use this shortcut. **Word 2000 »** Word 2000 doesn't include the Ctrl-Shift-R keyboard shortcut (or the ToolsWordCountRecount command that's linked to it in Word 2003 and Word XP).

Alt-Shift-F7

Display the Research task pane and activate the Translate feature

The Translate feature lets you translate the selection into a limited selection of other languages. **Word XP »** Word XP uses the Translate task pane for translation, not the Research task pane. **Word 2000 »** Word 2000 doesn't include the Translate feature.

Working with Tables

Word offers only a handful of keyboard shortcuts for working with tables, but most of them are well worth knowing.

Shortcuts for Working with Tables

Tab

Move to the next cell and select its contents

Press Tab to move to the next cell, automatically selecting its contents. (After pressing Tab, press ← to deselect the selection and move the insertion point to the beginning of the cell, or press → to deselect the selection and move the insertion point to the end of the cell.)

If the current cell is the last cell in the table, pressing Tab adds a new row to the table after the current last row and selects the first cell in the new row.

Shift-Tab

Move to the previous cell and select its contents

Press Shift-Tab to move to the previous cell, automatically selecting its contents. (After pressing Shift-Tab, press ← to deselect the selection and move the insertion point to the beginning of the cell, or press → to deselect the selection and move the insertion point to the end of the cell.)

Alt-5 on the numeric keypad, with NumLock off

Select all of the current table

Use this shortcut when you need to manipulate all of a table. You can also use it when you need to move quickly to the beginning or end of the table: select all the table, and then press ← to collapse the selection to the beginning of the table or → to collapse the selection to the end of the table.

Ctrl-Shift-Enter

Split the table at the insertion point

Click to place the insertion point at the beginning of the row where you want to split the table, and then press this shortcut. This shortcut is the equivalent of the Table | Split Table command.

>> *Tip: Use this shortcut (or the Split Table command) when a document has a table as its first item, and you need to insert paragraphs above the table.*

`Ctrl`-`Alt`-`U`

Update autoformatting on the selected table

You may need to update the autoformatting on a table after you add or delete rows, columns, or cells.

Performing Mail Merge

Word supports the following keyboard shortcuts for performing common mail-merge operations.

Shortcuts for Performing Mail Merge

`Alt`-`Shift`-`F`

Display the Insert Merge Field dialog box

Use the Insert Merge Field dialog box to insert a merge field in the mail-merge document.

`Alt`-`Shift`-`K`

Display the Checking and Reporting Errors dialog box

In the Checking and Reporting Errors dialog box, select the type of check you want to perform, and then click the OK button.

`Alt`-`Shift`-`E`

Open a mail-merge data source

If the active mail-merge document already has a data source attached, Word warns you that opening another data source will break the link to the current data source. Click the Break the Link button to proceed.

`Alt`-`Shift`-`N`

Display the Merge to New Document dialog box

In the Merge to New Document dialog box, choose which records to merge, and then click the OK button.

Alt - Shift - M

Display the Merge to Printer diaog box

In the Merge to Printer dialog box, choose which records to merge, and then click the OK button.

Customizing Word to Add Your Shortcuts

As you've seen so far in this chapter, Word comes with an impressive number of keyboard shortcuts already built in. But if you use Word extensively, you'll more than likely want to add keyboard shortcuts of your own or customize the built-in keyboard shortcuts. Word offers great flexibility here as well.

Understanding Where You Can Create Keyboard Shortcuts

You can create customized keyboard shortcuts in any document, any template, or in the Normal.dot global template. (Normal.dot is loaded all the time Word is running.) Here's how these three layers work:

- **Document**   A keyboard shortcut you create in a document works only when that document is active. A keyboard shortcut in a document overrides any keyboard shortcut that uses the same keys in the document's template or in the Normal template.

- **Template**   A keyboard shortcut you create in a template works when a document attached to that template is open or when the template itself is open. (Usually, you don't open a template directly except when you need to make changes to its contents. Instead, you work with documents based on the template.) The keyboard shortcut overrides any keyboard shortcut that uses the same keys in the Normal template but can itself be overridden by a keyboard shortcut in the attached document.

- **Normal.dot global template**   A keyboard shortcut you create in the Normal template works any time Word is running, except when a keyboard shortcut in the active document or the template attached to the active document overrides it.

>> Caution: *Windows shortcuts that you create for applications override Word shortcuts. For example, if you assign* Ctrl - Alt - W *to a Windows shortcut that runs Word, you can't use* Ctrl - Alt - W *in Word itself. (See "Creating Keyboard Shortcuts to Run Applications" in Chapter 2 for details of how to create such Windows shortcuts.)*

Being able to create keyboard shortcuts in three different layers gives you great flexibility, but it also means that when you create a shortcut, you must make sure you're putting it in the right place:

- If you want your shortcuts to be available whenever you're using Word, create them in Normal.dot.

- If you need a shortcut only in documents based on a particular template, create it in that template.

- If you need a shortcut only in a particular document, create it in that document.

Creating New Keyboard Shortcuts

To create a new keyboard shortcut in Word, follow these steps:

1. Choose Tools | Customize to display the Customize dialog box.

2. Click the Keyboard button on any of the three tabs to display the Customize Keyboard dialog box. Figure 4-2 shows the dialog box with an assignment under way so that you can see all the components of the dialog box.

Word 2000 » In Word 2000, the Customize Keyboard dialog box is a different shape but offers the same controls.

3. In the Save Changes In drop-down list, select the document or template to which you want to apply the keyboard shortcut.

4. In the Categories list box, select the category of item for which you want to create or change the keyboard shortcut. The list box to the right of the Categories list box changes its name to match the category you select.

   - Each of the eight menu categories (File, Edit, View, Insert, Format, Tools, Table, and Window and Help) lists the commands associated with that menu. The more commonly used commands appear on the menus, while the less-used commands don't appear. For example, the FilePrint command appears on the File menu as the Print command, but the FileConfirmConversions command doesn't appear.

   - The Drawing category lists the commands associated with the Drawing toolbar.

   - The Borders category lists the commands associated with the border buttons on the Tables and Borders toolbar.

   - The Mail Merge category lists the commands associated with the Tools | Letters and Mailings submenu (in Word 2003 and Word XP) and with the Mail Merge toolbar.

Word 2003

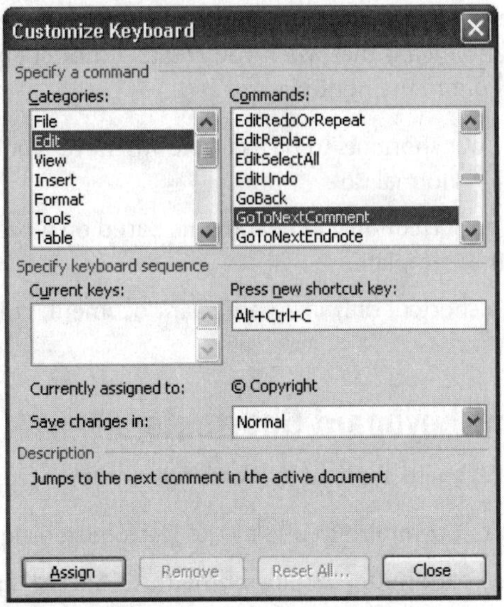

Figure 4-2

The Customize Keyboard dialog box lets you assign a keyboard shortcut to almost any command, macro, font, AutoText entry, style, or common symbol.

- The All Commands category lists all Word commands. Because there are so many commands, this list is awkward to use, so you'll probably want to use it only when you can't remember which menu a command is associated with.
- The Macros category lists all the macros available in the active document and templates.
- The Fonts category lists the fonts installed on Windows XP.
- The AutoText category lists the AutoText entries defined in Word.
- The Styles category lists the styles available in the active document and templates.
- The Common Symbols category lists frequently used symbols (such as em dashes, ® and © marks, and paragraph marks).

5. In the right-hand list box, select the command for which you want to create or change a keyboard shortcut. Word displays any existing keyboard shortcut for the command in the Current Keys list box.

6. Press [Alt]-[N] or click in the Press New Shortcut Key text box to put the focus there.

7. Press the keyboard shortcut you want to assign. If this shortcut is currently assigned to another command, Word displays the Currently Assigned To line listing the command, so that you'll know which existing shortcut you're about to overwrite. Choose a different keyboard shortcut if necessary.

8. Click the Assign button to assign the keyboard shortcut to the command.

9. Assign further keyboard shortcuts as necessary.

10. Click the Close button to close the Customize Keyboard dialog box.

11. Click the Close button to close the Customize dialog box.

After adding keyboard shortcuts, save the document or template, as discussed in "Saving Your Changes," a little later in this chapter.

Removing and Resetting Keyboard Shortcuts

To remove a keyboard shortcut, display the Customize Keyboard dialog box, specify which document or template you want to affect, and select the command so that Word displays the current keyboard shortcut. Select the shortcut in the Current Keys list box, and then click the Remove button.

To reset all keyboard shortcuts in the specified document or template to their default settings, click the Reset All button, and then click the Yes button in the confirmation dialog box:

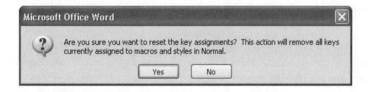

» Note: *The Reset All button isn't available until the document or template contains customized keyboard shortcuts.*

After removing or resetting keyboard shortcuts, save the document or template, as described next.

Saving Your Changes

After customizing keyboard shortcuts in a document, template, or Normal.dot, immediately save the file you customized to avoid losing the customization should Word or Windows crash:

- To save the document, issue a Save command by pressing Ctrl-S, clicking the Save button, or choosing File | Save as usual.

- To save the template attached to the document, issue a Save command for the document. Word then prompts you to save changes to the document template. Click the Yes button.

Word 2003

- To save changes to Normal.dot, press [Alt] to activate the menu bar, and then press [Shift]-[F] to display the File menu with the Save All command in place of the Save command. (Alternatively, hold down [Shift] as you click the File menu entry with the mouse.) Then choose the Save All item. Word saves the active document and prompts you to save changes to Normal.dot. Click the Yes button.

Using AutoText

As you saw in Chapter 3, AutoCorrect can help you enter text items of up to 255 characters in any of the Office applications. In Word, you can create formatted AutoCorrect entries as well, which can contain not only formatted text but also graphics.

Word also lets you create AutoText entries for inserting boilerplate text and graphics in your documents. AutoText entries are very similar to AutoCorrect entries, but they're not triggered automatically, so you can use standard words in their names.

Creating New AutoText Entries

To create an AutoText entry, follow these steps:

1. Create the contents of the AutoText entry in a document, and then select the material for the entry.

2. Press [Alt]-[F3] (or click the New button on the AutoText toolbar) to display the Create AutoText dialog box:

3. In the Please Name Your AutoText Entry text box, edit the default name that Word suggests. (The default name for AutoText entries you create this way consists of the first two words of the text—assuming the text has at least two words.)

4. Click the OK button to close the Create AutoText dialog box and create the AutoText entry.

Deleting AutoText Entries

To delete an AutoText entry, display the AutoText tab of the AutoCorrect dialog box (Tools | AutoCorrect Options, or Tools | AutoCorrect in Word 2000). Select the entry and click the Delete button.

From the AutoText tab of the AutoCorrect dialog box, you can also create an AutoText entry from the current selection by clicking the Add button, but it's usually easier to use the Create AutoText dialog box, as described a moment ago.

The most important option on the AutoText tab is the Show AutoComplete Suggestions check box, which controls whether Word displays a ScreenTip showing an available AutoText entry when you've typed enough letters to identify it. Clear this check box if you prefer to trigger your AutoText entries manually.

The Preview box helps you identify an AutoText entry that you can't identify by name. You can then click the Insert button to insert the entry at the insertion point.

Entering AutoText Entries

The standard way to enter an AutoText entry is to use the AutoComplete feature. When Word notices that you've typed the first few characters in an AutoText entry's name, it displays a ScreenTip showing the first few words so that you can identify it:

You can press Tab to enter the AutoText entry and continue typing in the same paragraph, or press Enter to enter the AutoText entry and start a new paragraph.

If you prefer not to use AutoComplete, you can enter an AutoText entry by typing enough letters to identify it and then pressing F3. (If nothing happens when you press F3, you haven't typed enough letters to uniquely identify the AutoText entry.)

You can also insert AutoText entries by using the Insert | AutoText submenu or the drop-down menu button on the AutoText toolbar.

Moving AutoText Entries from One Template to Another

AutoText entries are stored in templates. By default, Word stores all your AutoText entries in Normal.dot, the global template that's loaded whenever you start

Word 2003

Word. But you can copy or move AutoText entries from one template to another if necessary. Having all your AutoText entries in Normal.dot is convenient because it means they're always available when you're working in Word, no matter which template the active document is attached to. But if your AutoText entries are large (for example, if they contain graphics), Normal.dot will grow to a large file size, which can make Word run more slowly. In this case, it's a good idea to move any AutoText entries that apply only to a certain template to that template so that they're not slowing down Word.

You'll also need to store AutoText entries in their own templates if you want to make different AutoText entries available for different templates. When you do this, the AutoText entries in the template to which the active document is attached take precedence over the AutoText entries in Normal.dot.

To copy or move AutoText entries from one template to another, follow these steps:

1. Choose Tools | Templates and Add-Ins to display the Templates and Add-ins dialog box.

2. Click the Organizer button to display the Organizer dialog box.

3. Click the AutoText tab to display it.

4. If necessary, use the Close File button and the resulting Open File button on either side of the AutoText tab to open and close the templates you want to work with.

5. In the list box for the source template, select the AutoText entry.

6. Click the Copy button to copy it to the other template.

7. If you want to remove the AutoText entry from the source template, click the Delete button.

8. After copying or moving all the AutoText entries you want to affect, click the Close button to close the Organizer dialog box.

9. Save both templates involved.

Excel 2003 Keyboard Shortcuts

Excel supports a good variety of keyboard shortcuts that can save you a lot of time and hand movement. If you work with the keyboard shortcuts a little, you'll quickly learn which ones benefit you most in your day-to-day work. Some are natural candidates for everyday use, while others are more esoteric.

How much you use the keyboard in Excel is likely to depend on the tasks you're performing. For example, if you need to manipulate elements in a chart, you'll probably find that you use the mouse more than the keyboard.

Notes on the Standard Shortcuts

Excel supports the standard Office keyboard shortcuts discussed in "Shared Keyboard Shortcuts" in Chapter 3. The following exceptions are worth noting.

Creating a New Default Workbook

Ctrl-N

Create a new default workbook

The new default workbook uses Excel's default settings for font, cell height and width, alignment, and so on. You can customize these default settings for new workbooks by creating a workbook named Book.xlt in the %*userprofile*%\ Application Data\Microsoft\Excel\XLSTART\ folder. (%*userprofile*% is a variable that returns to the folder that contains your Windows XP user profile.) Open Book.xlt and change the settings in it to suit your preferences.

Minimizing and Navigating Among Workbooks

Unlike Word and PowerPoint, Excel keeps all the open workbooks inside the same application window. This means that when you minimize a workbook, it's minimized within the Excel window rather than simply minimized to the

Windows taskbar. So Excel offers keyboard shortcuts for working with minimized workbooks.

>> **Note:** *Another way to access a minimized workbook is to click its button in the Windows taskbar—if the window has a button. You can choose whether to display one taskbar button for each open workbook (choose Tools | Options and select the Windows in Taskbar check box on the View tab of the Options dialog box) or just one taskbar button for the Excel application itself (clear the Windows in Taskbar check box).*

Ctrl - F9

Minimize the active workbook window

Minimizing a workbook window shrinks it to a title bar icon at the bottom of the Excel window:

Ctrl - Tab

Select the next minimized workbook window

Use the Ctrl-Tab keyboard shortcut to select the next minimized workbook window so that you can restore or maximize it by using Ctrl-F10.

Ctrl - Shift - Tab

Select the previous minimized workbook window

Use the Ctrl-Shift-Tab keyboard shortcut to select the previous minimized workbook window so that you can restore or maximize it by using Ctrl-F10.

Ctrl - F10

Restore or maximize the selected minimized workbook window

Use Ctrl-Tab or Ctrl-Shift-Tab to select a workbook window so that you can restore or maximize it using this keyboard shortcut.

Navigating in Worksheets

Unless your workbooks consist of a single worksheet with only a few cells on it, you'll spend a fair amount of time navigating your worksheets in Excel. Keyboard shortcuts can save you a large amount of scrolling and clicking with the mouse.

Shortcuts for Navigating in Worksheets

[←], [→], [↑], [↓]

Move the active cell up or down one row, or left or right one column

Use the arrow keys for basic navigation. For example, press [→] to move the active cell highlight to the cell to the right of the current active cell. Hold down the arrow key to move through multiple cells.

[Shift]-[F11], [Alt]-[Shift]-[F1]

Insert a new worksheet in the active workbook

These keyboard shortcuts make Excel insert a new default worksheet.

[Ctrl]-[Page Down]

Move to the next worksheet

[Ctrl]-[Page Up]

Move to the previous worksheet

[Ctrl]-[Shift]-[Page Down]

Select the current worksheet and the next worksheet

[Ctrl]-[Shift]-[Page Up]

Select the current worksheet and the previous worksheet

[Ctrl]-[←], [Ctrl]-[→], [Ctrl]-[↑], [Ctrl]-[↓]

Move to the specified edge of the data region

The data region is the area of the active worksheet that contains the active cell and has cells that contain data. The data region extends from the active cell to the nearest blank row above and below, and to the nearest blank column to the left and right. For example, if a worksheet contains entries from cell D8 through K23, the data region starts at cell D8 and extends to row 23 and column K. Pressing [Ctrl]-[→] moves the active cell to column K in the active row. Pressing

Ctrl-↓ moves the active cell to row 23 in the active column. Pressing Ctrl-←
returns the active cell to column D, and pressing Ctrl-↑ returns the active cell
to row 8.

Home

Move to the first cell in the active row

Use this keyboard shortcut to move the active cell from the far reaches of the
worksheet to the first column. This keyboard shortcut is especially useful when
you need to check row headings that are not displayed.

Ctrl-Home

Move to the first cell in the worksheet

Ctrl-End

Move to the last used cell in the worksheet

Page Down

Move down one screen

Page Up

Move up one screen

Alt-Page Down

Move to the right by one screen

Alt-Page Up

Move to the left by one screen

Ctrl-Backspace

Scroll the workbook to display the active cell

Ctrl-G

Display the Go To dialog box

The Go To dialog box (shown next) lets you quickly access the named ranges in
the active worksheet. You can also press Alt-S from the Go To dialog box to

display the Go To Special dialog box (shown on the right), which lets you access cells that meet specific criteria.

Go To   [?][X]

Go to:

Capital
DailyRate
Interest
Term1
Term2

Reference:

|

[Special...]   [OK]   [Cancel]

Go To Special   [X]

Select
○ Comments   ○ Row differences
○ Constants   ○ Column differences
◉ Formulas   ○ Precedents
  ☑ Numbers   ○ Dependents
  ☑ Text   ⊙ Direct only
  ☑ Logicals   ○ All levels
  ☑ Errors   ○ Last cell
○ Blanks   ○ Visible cells only
○ Current region   ○ Conditional formats
○ Current array   ○ Data validation
○ Objects   ⊙ All
                       ○ Same

[OK]   [Cancel]

Selecting Cells, Rows, and Columns

To select a range of cells with the mouse, you simply click and drag. (To select a single cell, simply click it.) Alternatively, click to select the first cell, hold down [Shift], and then click the last cell to select the range in between. You can also select cells, rows, and columns with the keyboard by using the following keyboard shortcuts.

Shortcuts for Selecting Cells, Rows, and Columns

[Shift]-[←], [Shift]-[→], [Shift]-[↑], [Shift]-[↓]

Extend the selection in the direction of the arrow key

Hold down [Shift] and use the arrow keys to extend the selection by as many rows and columns as necessary.

[Ctrl]-[Spacebar]

Select the current column

[Shift]-[Spacebar]

Select the current row

[Ctrl]-[A]

Select all cells on the current worksheet

Shift - Backspace

Reduce the selection to the active cell

If the active cell is off the screen, Excel scrolls the window so that the active cell is displayed. If multiple cells are selected, Excel reduces the selection to the active cell and scrolls the window so that the active cell is displayed.

Ctrl - Shift - Spacebar

Select all the objects on the current worksheet while retaining the current selection

F8

Toggle Extend mode on and off

Press F8 to turn on Extend mode, and then use the arrow keys and other navigation keys without Shift to select a range. Excel displays EXT on the status bar when Extend mode is on. Press F8 again to turn off Extend mode.

Shift - F8

Toggle Add mode on and off

Turn on Add mode so that you can add another range of cells to the existing selection. Press Shift-F8, and then use the arrow keys and other navigation keys without Shift to select each further range as necessary. Excel displays ADD on the status bar when Add mode is on. Press Shift-F8 again to turn off Add mode.

Ctrl - Shift - ←, Ctrl - Shift - →, Ctrl - Shift - ↑, Ctrl - Shift - ↓

Extend the selection to the first or last cell in the data area

The data area is a block of cells containing entries. The end of the data area is defined by a blank column at the left or right, and by a blank row at the top or bottom. Pressing Ctrl-Shift-↑ and Ctrl-Shift-↓ in this shortcut extends the selection to the first or last row in the data area. Pressing Ctrl-Shift-← and Ctrl-Shift-→ extends the selection to the first or last column in the data area. For example, press Ctrl-Shift-→ to extend the selection to the last column used in the data area for the row containing the active cell.

Shift - Home

Extend the selection to the first cell in the row

Ctrl-Shift-Home

Extend the selection to the first cell in the worksheet

Ctrl-Shift-End

Extend the selection to the last cell used on the worksheet

The last cell used is the last cell that has ever contained an entry. It may not currently contain an entry.

End, then Shift-←, Shift-→, Shift-↑, Shift-↓

Extend the selection to the last cell with contents in the active column or row

End, then Shift-Home

Extend the selection to the last cell with contents on the worksheet

End, then Shift-Enter

Extend the selection to the last cell in the active row

Shift-Page Down

Extend the selection downward by one screen

Shift-Page Up

Extend the selection upward by one screen

Scroll Lock, then Shift-Home

Extend the selection to the first cell in the window

Depending on your keyboard, you may need to press Scroll Lock again to switch it off after using this keyboard shortcut and the next.

Scroll Lock, then Shift-End

Extend the selection to the last cell in the window

Selecting Cells That Match Criteria

Beyond the shortcuts for general selection discussed in the previous section, Excel offers shortcuts for more specialized selection—for example, selecting the cells referenced by a formula, or selecting cells in a row or column whose value is different from the value in the active cell.

Shortcuts for Selecting Cells That Match Criteria

Ctrl-Shift-*, Ctrl-* on the numeric keypad

Select the data region

The data region is a block of cells containing entries. The end of the data area is defined by a blank column at the left or right, and by a blank row at the top or bottom.

Ctrl-/

Select the array that the active cell is in

Ctrl-\

Select nonmatching cells in the active row

This shortcut selects cells in the active row whose values don't match the value in the active cell.

Ctrl-Shift-|

Select nonmatching cells in the active column

This shortcut selects cells in the active column whose values don't match the value in the active cell.

Ctrl-Shift-O

Select all cells that have comments attached

This shortcut uses the letter O, not zero.

Alt-;

Select only the visible cells in the current selection

This shortcut is useful when the selected area contains hidden rows or columns that you don't want to include when copying the contents of the selected area. (If you select the whole area, Excel includes any hidden rows or columns. These rows and columns appear when you paste the data.)

Ctrl-[

Select cells directly referenced by formulas in the active cell

`Ctrl`-`[]`

Select cells that contain formulas directly referencing the active cell

`Ctrl`-`Shift`-`{}`

Select cells directly or indirectly referenced by formulas in the active cell

`Ctrl`-`Shift`-`{}`

Select cells that contain formulas directly or indirectly referencing the active cell

Entering and Editing Data

Excel provides the following keyboard shortcuts for entering data in your worksheets and editing the existing entries in cells. To start entering data in a blank cell, simply select the cell and type the entry.

Shortcuts for Entering and Editing Data

`Enter`

Enter the entry in the cell and select the next cell

By default, when you press `Enter`, Excel selects the next cell below the active cell. You can change the direction of the next cell (up, down, left, or right), or turn off the movement, by using the Move Selection After Enter check box and Direction drop-down list on the Edit tab of the Options dialog box (Tools | Options).

`Esc`

Cancel editing in the active cell

Canceling editing loses any changes you've made to the cell's contents.

`Shift`-`Enter`

Enter the entry in the cell and select the next cell in the opposite direction

Press `Shift`-`Enter` to select the cell in the opposite direction from that specified in the Direction drop-down list on the Edit tab of the Options dialog box.

`Tab`

Enter the entry in the cell and select the next cell to the right

`Shift`-`Tab`

Enter the entry in the cell and select the next cell to the left

Ctrl-Enter

Fill the selected range with the entry

Select the range of cells you want to affect, type the entry, and press Ctrl-Enter to enter it in all the cells simultaneously.

Ctrl-Shift-:

Enter the time in the active cell

Ctrl-;

Enter the date in the active cell

Ctrl-F3

Display the Define Name dialog box

Use the Define Name dialog box (shown here) to add and delete range names.

Ctrl-Shift-F3

Display the Create Names dialog box

Use the Create Names dialog box (shown here) to create names from row labels and column labels.

Alt - ↓

Display the AutoComplete drop-down list

The AutoComplete drop-down list shows the entries in the column available for reuse.

Amsterdam
Barcelona
Berlin
Chicago
Glasgow
London
Memphis
Porto

F2

Switch the active cell into Edit mode

To edit the existing contents of a cell, select it and press F2. Excel places the insertion point at the end of the cell's existing contents.

>> Note: *If the Edit Directly in Cell check box on the Edit tab of the Options dialog box is cleared, pressing F2 activates the Formula bar instead.*

Shift - F2

Insert a new comment or edit the existing comment

If the active cell has a comment attached to it, Excel opens the comment for editing. If the active cell has no comment, Excel creates a new comment.

Backspace

Delete the contents of the active cell

Pressing Backspace deletes the contents of the active cell when the cell is *not* in Edit mode.

Ctrl - Delete

Delete from the insertion point to the end of the cell's contents

Press F2 to switch the cell to Edit mode, position the insertion point after the last character you want to keep, and then press this shortcut to delete the rest.

Alt - Enter

Begin a new line within the active cell

Use this shortcut when you need to break text to a new line within a cell.

Ctrl - Shift - Z

Undo the most recent AutoCorrect

This shortcut works only when Excel is displaying the AutoCorrect Smart Tag.

Excel 2000 » Excel 2000 doesn't support Smart Tags, so it doesn't offer this shortcut.

Ctrl - 6

Cycle object display, placeholder display, and hiding

Press Ctrl - 6 to cycle between displaying objects, displaying placeholders for objects, and hiding objects.

Inserting and Deleting Cells

To change the contents and layout of your worksheets, you'll often need to insert extra cells or delete existing cells. Excel provides keyboard shortcuts for both operations.

Shortcuts for Inserting and Deleting Cells

Ctrl - -

Delete the selected cells

If you have one or more cells selected, Excel displays the Delete cells dialog box (shown here) so that you can specify in which direction to move the remaining cells. You can also choose to delete the row or column. If you press this shortcut with one or more rows or columns selected, Excel deletes the rows or columns without confirmation.

Ctrl - Shift - +

Insert cells

Excel displays the Insert cells dialog box (shown here) so that you can choose whether to move the other cells to the right or down. You can also choose to insert an entire row or column. If you press this shortcut with one or more rows or columns selected, Excel inserts the same number of rows or columns without displaying the Insert cells dialog box.

Working with Formulas

If you construct your own worksheets, you'll probably spend a fair amount of time working with formulas. If you type those formulas, you'll be glad to know that Excel provides plenty of keyboard shortcuts for working with formulas.

Shortcuts for Working with Formulas

`=`

Start creating a formula

You can also start creating a formula by typing + or -, but = is the standard way of starting a formula.

`Enter`

Enter the formula in the cell

After you've completed the formula, press `Enter` to enter it in the cell. Pressing `Enter` is the equivalent of clicking the Enter button, and usually much more convenient.

`Ctrl`-`Shift`-`Enter`

Enter the formula as an array formula

An array formula is a formula that works on a range of cells (an *array*) to perform multiple calculations that generate either a single result or multiple results. Excel displays braces ({}) around an array formula to identify it.

`Ctrl`-`` ` ``

Toggle between displaying formula results and formulas

By default, Excel displays formula results in cells. You can display the formulas themselves by pressing this shortcut or by selecting the Formulas check box on the View tab of the Options dialog box (Tools | Options). Note that the key is the single quote mark (`` ` ``), not the apostrophe.

`Shift`-`F3`

Display the Insert Function dialog box

When working in a formula, press this shortcut to display the Insert Function dialog box so that you can insert a function in a formula.

`Ctrl`-`A`

Display the Function Arguments dialog box

When constructing a formula, move the insertion point to just after a function name, and then press this shortcut to display the Function Arguments dialog box, which walks you through supplying the correct arguments for the function.

Ctrl - Shift - A

Enter the argument names in the Formula bar

When constructing a formula, move the insertion point to just after a function name, and then press this shortcut to enter the argument names as placeholders in the Formula bar:

Excel then moves the highlight along as you replace each placeholder in turn with valid data or a valid reference.

F3

Displays the Paste Name dialog box

Use the Paste Name dialog box (shown here) to enter an existing range name. You can type the name manually if you prefer, but the dialog box can be useful for getting complex names correct and for reminding yourself of range names you've forgotten. (If you haven't defined any range names, Excel doesn't display the Paste Name dialog box when you press F3.)

Alt-**=**

Insert an AutoSum formula in the active cell

 Pressing this shortcut is the equivalent of clicking the AutoSum button on the Standard toolbar.

Ctrl-**Shift**-**"**

Copy the value of the cell above the active cell

This shortcut makes Excel copy the value from the cell above the active cell into the active cell.

Ctrl-**'**

Copy the formula from the cell above the active cell

This shortcut makes Excel copy the formula from the cell above the active cell into the active cell.

Recalculating Worksheets and Workbooks

Excel normally recalculates all cells in a workbook automatically when the value in any cell changes. But if you work with complex workbooks, you may need to turn off automatic recalculation (on the Calculation tab of the Options dialog box) to prevent lengthy recalculation from slowing down your work. You can then force recalculation manually when needed by using the following keyboard shortcuts.

Shortcuts for Recalculating Worksheets and Workbooks

F9

Recalculate all the worksheets in all the open workbooks

This command recalculates all the cells that have changed and the cells they affect. If the workbooks are highly complex, recalculation may take a long time.

Shift-**F9**

Recalculate the active worksheet only

If your changes are limited to the active worksheet, use this shortcut to restrict recalculation to that worksheet.

Ctrl-**Alt**-**F9**

Recalculate all calculations in all the worksheets in all the open workbooks

This command recalculates even cells that have not changed. You shouldn't need to use it often.

`Ctrl`-`Alt`-`Shift`-`F9`

Recheck all formulas, then recalculate all calculations in all the worksheets

This "Vulcan Nerve Pinch" four-key shortcut is the ultimate in recalculation: Excel rechecks all formulas in all the worksheets in the open workbooks, then recalculates all the cells, even those that have not changed.

Formatting Cells

Excel provides a wide range of formatting for both the contents of cells and their appearance so that the cells show exactly the data you want, in the right format, and with the appropriate emphasis. You can apply most cell formatting using the keyboard.

Shortcuts for Formatting Cells

`Alt`-`'`

Display the Style dialog box

`Ctrl`-`1`

Display the Format Cells dialog box

This shortcut works only with the 1 key in the key row, not the 1 key on the keypad.

`Ctrl`-`Shift`-`~`

Apply the General format

`Ctrl`-`Shift`-`$`

Apply the two-decimal-place Currency format

`Ctrl`-`Shift`-`%`

Apply the Percentage format (no decimal places)

`Ctrl`-`Shift`-`^`

Apply the Exponential format with two decimal places

`Ctrl`-`Shift`-`#`

Apply the DD-MMM-YY date format

Excel 2003

[Ctrl]-[Shift]-[@]

Apply the HH:MM AM/PM time format

[Ctrl]-[Shift]-[!]

Apply the two-decimal-place number format with the thousands separator

[Ctrl]-[5]

Toggle strikethrough

Applying Borders

Excel includes two shortcuts for applying and removing an outline border by using the keyboard.

[Ctrl]-[Shift]-[&]

Apply an outline border

[Ctrl]-[Shift]-[_]

Remove the outline border

For more complex borders, press [Ctrl]-[1], and then use the Borders tab of the Format Cells dialog box (Figure 5-1). This tab is largely graphical, but you can also manipulate its border controls by using [Alt]-based keyboard shortcuts. Unlike most dialog box shortcuts, these shortcuts aren't marked with underscores, so most people don't know about them.

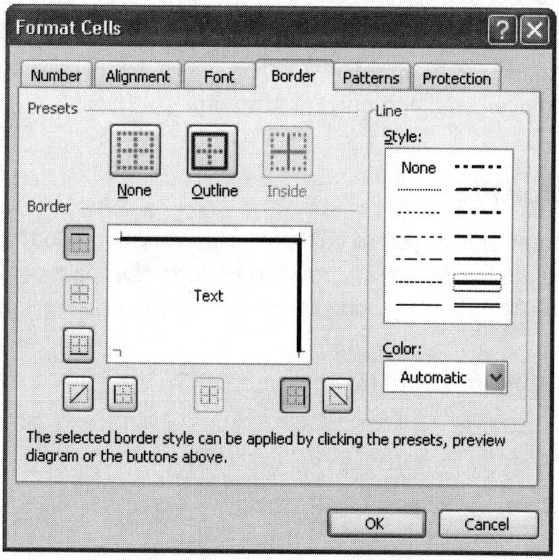

Figure 5-1
You can use [Alt]-based shortcuts to manipulate the border controls on the Border tab of the Format Cells dialog box.

[Alt]-[T]

Toggle the top border on the selected cells

[Alt]-[B]

Toggle the bottom border on the selected cells

[Alt]-[L]

Toggle the left border on the selected cells

[Alt]-[R]

Toggle the right border on the selected cells

[Alt]-[D]

Toggle the downward diagonal border on the selected cells

[Alt]-[U]

Toggle the upward diagonal border on the selected cells

[Alt]-[H]

Toggle the horizontal border on the selected cells

[Alt]-[V]

Toggle the vertical border on the selected cells

You can also use the access keys that *are* displayed on the Borders tab: [Alt]-[N] to apply the None preset, [Alt]-[O] to apply the Outline preset, [Alt]-[I] to apply the Inside preset (to a multicell selection only), and so on.

Working in Outlines

Excel's outlining features enable you to collapse large worksheets so that only the parts you need to see appear on screen. You can perform the main outlining actions easily from the keyboard by using the shortcuts described in this section.

Shortcuts for Working in Outlines

[Alt]-[Shift]-[→]

Group the selected rows or columns

Alt - Shift - ←

Ungroup the selected rows or columns

Ctrl - 8

Toggle the display of outline symbols

You can hide outline symbols to reclaim the space that they take up on screen. Redisplay the symbols when you need to work with them again.

Hiding and Unhiding Rows and Columns

Excel provides shortcuts for quickly hiding and unhiding rows and columns from the keyboard. To hide rows or columns, select them before pressing the shortcut. To unhide rows or columns, select cells in the rows or columns around them, and then press the shortcut.

Shortcuts for Hiding and Unhiding Rows and Columns

Ctrl - 9

Hide all selected rows

Ctrl - 0

Hide all selected columns

Ctrl - Shift - ((

Unhide hidden rows in the selection

Ctrl - Shift - ()

Unhide hidden columns in the selection

Creating and Navigating in Charts

Charts are a quintessentially graphical item, but Excel also provides a couple of keyboard shortcuts worth knowing. You can access a chart sheet just as you would any other worksheet, by pressing Ctrl - Page Down (to move to the next worksheet) or Ctrl - Page Up (to move to the previous worksheet) until the chart sheet is selected.

Shortcuts for Creating and Navigating in Charts

[F11], [Alt]-[F1]

Create a chart from the selected range

This shortcut creates a chart using the default chart type. If you often create charts of the same type, you can customize the default chart setting. To do so, follow these steps:

1. Right-click a chart and choose Chart Type from the shortcut menu to display the Chart Type dialog box. Alternatively, select the chart and choose Chart | Chart Type.

2. Select the chart type on the Standard Types tab or the Custom Types tab.

3. Click the Set as Default Chart button. Excel displays a confirmation dialog box.

4. Click the Yes button.

5. Click the OK button to close the Chart Type dialog box.

[←], [→], [↑], [↓]

Select the next chart component in the direction of the arrow

With a chart component selected, you can press [←], [→], [↑], or [↓] to move the selection to another component. For example, press [→] to select the next item to the right of the currently selected item.

Working in PivotTables

Like charts, PivotTables are largely graphical items for which the mouse tends to be much more convenient than the keyboard. Nevertheless, if you work extensively with PivotTables, you may benefit from knowing the keyboard shortcuts that Excel offers for working with them.

Shortcuts for Working in PivotTables

[Ctrl]-[Shift]-[*]

Select the entire PivotTable

When you want to take an action with the PivotTable—for example, apply formatting to it—use this shortcut to select the whole PivotTable.

[Alt]-[Shift]-[→]

Group the selected items

Select the items you want to group, and then press this shortcut.

`Alt`-`Shift`-`←`

Ungroup the grouped items

Select the group of items, and then press this shortcut to ungroup the items.

`←`, `→`, `↑`, `↓`

Navigate from item to item in the PivotTable

Working in Data Forms

To help you enter data in a database more easily, Excel offers *data forms*—custom dialog boxes that Excel creates using the fields that make up the database. Excel provides keyboard shortcuts for navigating within and among data forms.

Shortcuts for Working in Data Forms

`Ctrl`-`Page Down`

Insert a new, blank record in the database

`Enter`

Move to the next record, first field

`Shift`-`Enter`

Move to the previous record, first field

`↓`

Move to the next record, same field

Excel selects the same field in the next record that was active in the current record.

`↑`

Move to the previous record, same field

Excel selects the same field in the previous record that was active in the current record.

`Page Down`

Move ten records forward, same field

Page Up

Move ten records backward, same field

Working in Print Preview

Print Preview is easy to navigate with the mouse, but you can also navigate effectively with the keyboard if you know which keys to press.

Shortcuts for Working in Print Preview

Ctrl - ↑

Display to the first page of the print area

This shortcut works only when Print Preview is zoomed out.

Ctrl - ↓

Display the last page of the print area

This shortcut works only when Print Preview is zoomed out.

Page Up

Display the previous page

This shortcut works only when Print Preview is zoomed out.

Page Down

Display the next page

This shortcut works only when Print Preview is zoomed out.

←, →, ↑, ↓

Move around the page

These shortcuts work only when Print Preview is zoomed in.

6

PowerPoint 2003 Keyboard Shortcuts

Although PowerPoint is a relatively visual application, you can take many actions in it
by using the keyboard. PowerPoint supports keyboard shortcuts for creating the text
of presentations, formatting it, spell-checking it, and for running presentations. As
you might expect, PowerPoint lacks shortcuts for its most graphical features, such
as creating, positioning, and formatting AutoShapes. For working with graphical
objects, you're much better off using the mouse.

Notes on the Standard Shortcuts

PowerPoint supports the standard Office
keyboard shortcuts discussed in "Shared
Keyboard Shortcuts" in Chapter 3. The
following exceptions are worth noting.

Shortcuts for Creating a New
Presentation

Ctrl-N

*Display the New Presentation pane or create
a new presentation*

Pressing Ctrl-N in PowerPoint 2003
displays the Slide Layout pane (shown
here), in which you can choose the type of
presentation to create. In PowerPoint XP
and PowerPoint 2000, pressing Ctrl-N
creates a new, blank presentation.

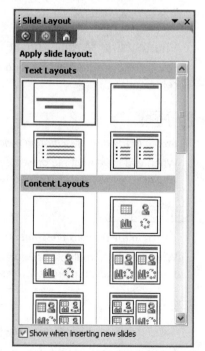

Shortcuts for Moving and Resizing Windows

Ctrl - Shift - F10

Activate the menu bar

In most cases, it's easier to press F10, the standard shortcut for activating the menu bar, than to use this triple bucky.

Shortcuts for Maximizing and Restoring the PowerPoint Window

PowerPoint supports two extra shortcuts for maximizing and restoring the PowerPoint window.

Alt - F10

Maximize the application window

You can use this shortcut instead of clicking the Maximize button on the PowerPoint window.

Alt - F5

Restore the application window

You can use this shortcut instead of clicking the Restore Down button on the PowerPoint window.

Shortcuts for Moving Among Presentation Windows and Panes

You can move among presentation windows and panes by using the following commands.

Ctrl - F6

Switch to the next presentation window

When you have multiple presentations open, you can use this keyboard shortcut to quickly access the next presentation.

Ctrl - Shift - F6

Switch to the previous presentation window

When you have multiple presentations open, you can use this keyboard shortcut to quickly access the previous presentation.

F6

Switch to the next pane in a clockwise direction

Use this shortcut and the next to move from pane to pane in the PowerPoint window.

`Shift`-`F6`

Switch to the next pane in a counterclockwise direction

Creating a Presentation

When creating a presentation, you can use the keyboard shortcuts that PowerPoint offers for selecting placeholders, inserting new slides and duplicating existing slides, toggling Print Preview, searching for the next instance of the current search term, and finding the next spelling error.

Shortcuts for Creating a Presentation and Its Contents

`Ctrl`-`Enter`

Select the next title placeholder or body text placeholder, or insert a new slide

Use this shortcut to move from one placeholder to another with the keyboard. When the currently selected placeholder is the last placeholder on a slide, pressing this shortcut inserts a new slide in the presentation after the active slide.

`Ctrl`-`M`

Insert a new slide

This shortcut is the equivalent of choosing Insert | New Slide.

`Ctrl`-`D`

Duplicate the selected slide

Duplicate a slide when you need to base another slide on it.

`Ctrl`-`F2`

Toggle Print Preview

`Shift`-`F4`

Search for the next instance of the current search term

After performing a search and closing the Find dialog box, you can find the next instance of the same search term by pressing this shortcut.

`Alt`-`F7`

Find the next spelling error

This shortcut is great for quickly moving from one apparent spelling error to the next in a presentation.

PowerPoint 2003

Working on the Outline for a Presentation

Because the outline for a presentation consists of text, you can save time when working on an outline by using the keyboard shortcuts that PowerPoint provides. You can use these shortcuts either when the focus is in the Outlining pane or when the focus is in a paragraph on a slide.

Shortcuts for Working on Outlines

[Alt]-[Shift]-[←]

Promote the active paragraph to the next level

For example, click in a heading level 2 paragraph and press this shortcut to promote the paragraph to heading level 1.

[Alt]-[Shift]-[→]

Demote the active paragraph to the next level

[Alt]-[Shift]-[↑]

Move the selected paragraphs up by one displayed item

This shortcut and the next move the selection by one displayed item at a time. If a slide is collapsed, it counts as one item; if it is expanded, it counts as multiple items. Either expand or collapse the outline before pressing this shortcut, or use the shortcut multiple times.

[Alt]-[Shift]-[↓]

Move the selected paragraphs down by one displayed item

[Alt]-[Shift]-[1]

Show heading level 1

This shortcut collapses the outline to display only heading level 1 paragraphs.

[Alt]-[Shift]-[+]

Expand the headings and text below the selected heading

Select a heading and press this shortcut to expand all the headings and text below it.

[Alt]-[Shift]-[-]

Collapse the headings and text below the selected heading

Select a heading and press this shortcut to collapse all the headings and text below it.

[Alt]-[Shift]-[A]

Toggle the display of all text and headings

Press this shortcut to quickly expand all slides to show their text and headings or collapse them to show only heading level 1 paragraphs.

[/]

Toggle the display of formatting in the Outlining pane

In PowerPoint 2000, you can press [/] (the forward slash key) on the numeric keypad to toggle the display of formatting in the Outlining pane. PowerPoint 2003 and PowerPoint XP don't support this keyboard shortcut.

Applying Formatting

To make any presentation look not only good but also powerful, convincing, or persuasive, you'll need to format its text and objects carefully. You can do much (sometimes all) of your formatting work from the keyboard.

Shortcuts for Applying Formatting

[Ctrl]-[Shift]-[F]

Select the Font drop-down list on the Formatting toolbar

[Ctrl]-[Shift]-[P]

Select the Font Size drop-down list on the Formatting toolbar

[Ctrl]-[Shift]-[>]

Increase the font size in jumps

[Ctrl]-[Shift]-[<]

Decrease the font size in jumps

Ctrl-T

Display the Font dialog box

Shift-F3

Cycle the case of the selection

This shortcut cycles the case among lowercase, title case (the first letter of each word is capitalized), and uppercase (all letters are capitalized). This shortcut is an alternative to the Format | Change Case command, but that command also offers a Sentence Case option (the first letter of each sentence is capitalized) and a tOGGLE cASE command (PowerPoint inverts the capitalization of each letter).

Ctrl-=

Toggle subscript

Subscript decreases the font size of the selected text and lowers it below the baseline of the other characters.

≫ Note: *The Superscript and Subscript check boxes and Offset text box in the Effects group box in the Font dialog box (Ctrl-T) give you more precise control over subscripts and superscripts.*

Ctrl-+

Toggle superscript

Superscript decreases the font size of the selected text and raises it above the baseline of the other characters.

Ctrl-Spacebar

Reset the formatting of the current paragraph or selection

Use this shortcut to quickly remove direct formatting that you've applied to text.

Ctrl-Shift-C

Copy the formatting of the selection

 Pressing this keyboard shortcut is the equivalent of clicking the Format Painter button on the Standard toolbar: it copies the formatting of the selected text or other object to the Clipboard, so that you can paste it to other text (or another object).

Ctrl-Shift-V

Apply the copied formatting to the selection

After copying formatting using Ctrl-Shift-C (or by clicking the Format Painter button), apply the formatting to its destination by using this shortcut or by clicking the Format Painter button.

Ctrl-J

Apply justified alignment to the paragraph

Applying justified alignment to (or "justifying") a paragraph aligns the left end of its lines with the left margin and the right end of its lines with the right margin. The last line isn't aligned with the right margin unless it happens to reach the margin anyway.

Shortcuts for Grouping and Ungrouping Items

Ctrl-Shift-G

Group the selected objects

Ctrl-Shift-H

Ungroup the selected group

Shortcuts for Displaying the Grid and Guides

Shift-F9

Toggle the display of the grid

Alt-F9

Toggle the display of guides

Ctrl-G

Display the Grid and Guides dialog box

Running a Slide Show

Most presenters stick with the mouse when giving their presentations, which works fine for advancing the presentation but leaves them stuck fumbling with the context menu and its submenus when they need to execute any other command. If you put in the modicum of effort required to learn the keyboard shortcuts that PowerPoint provides for running a slide show, you can control the presentation faster and more easily, which gives a more professional appearance to your presentation.

PowerPoint 2003

Shortcuts for Running a Slide Show

[F5]

Start a slide show

Press this shortcut instead of choosing Slide Show | View Show.

[Shift]-[F5]

Start a slide show from the current slide

Navigate to the slide from which you want to start the slide show, and then press this shortcut. Alternatively, click the Slide Show from Current Slide button on the horizontal scroll bar.

[Esc], [Ctrl]-[Break], [-] on the numeric keypad

End the slide show

[Esc] is the easiest shortcut for ending a presentation.

[N], [Enter], [Spacebar], [↓], [→], [Page Down]

Display the next animation or the next slide

Press any of these keys to trigger the next animation (if there is one) or display the next slide (if there is no further animation).

[P], [Backspace], [↑], [←], [Page Up]

Display the previous animation or the previous slide

Press any of these keys to trigger the previous animation (if there is one) or display the previous slide (if there is no previous animation).

[Ctrl]-[S]

Display the All Slides dialog box

Use the All Slides dialog box to navigate to a slide by its title.

<*number*>-[Enter]

Display the slide identified by the number

For example, press [5] [Enter] to display slide 5 in the presentation.

⬚B⬚, ⬚.⬚

Toggle a black screen

Press ⬚B⬚ or ⬚.⬚ to display a black screen in place of the current slide. Press ⬚B⬚ or ⬚.⬚ again to display the slide again.

⬚W⬚, ⬚,⬚

Toggle a white screen

Press ⬚W⬚ or ⬚,⬚ to display a white screen in place of the current slide. Press ⬚W⬚ or ⬚,⬚ again to display the slide again.

⬚S⬚, ⬚+⬚

Stop or restart an automatic slide show

If you've set a slide show to run automatically, press ⬚S⬚ or ⬚+⬚ to stop or restart it.

⬚Ctrl⬚-⬚P⬚

Change the pointer to a pen

You can use the pen to make annotations on the screen.

⬚Ctrl⬚-⬚A⬚

Change the pen back to the pointer

Use this shortcut to restore the pointer after making annotations.

⬚Ctrl⬚-⬚M⬚

Toggle the display of ink markup

⬚Ctrl⬚-⬚E⬚

Change the pointer to the eraser

⬚E⬚

Erase all on-screen annotations

Use this shortcut to erase any annotations you've made using the pen.

⬚H⬚

Display the next hidden slide

Use hidden slides to keep extra information up your sleeve.

PowerPoint 2003

$\boxed{\text{T}}$

Apply new timings while rehearsing

$\boxed{\text{O}}$

Use your original timings while rehearsing

$\boxed{\text{M}}$

Toggle to using the mouse to advance while rehearsing

$\boxed{\text{🖰}}$ both mouse buttons for two seconds

Return to the first slide

This isn't a keyboard shortcut, but it's well worth knowing as the quickest way to return to the first slide in the presentation.

$\boxed{\text{A}}$

Toggle hiding the pointer

$\boxed{\text{Ctrl}}$-$\boxed{\text{H}}$

Hide the pointer and button

$\boxed{\text{Ctrl}}$-$\boxed{\text{U}}$

Hide the pointer arrow for 15 seconds

$\boxed{\text{Shift}}$-$\boxed{\text{F10}}$ (or right-click)

Display the shortcut menu

After displaying the shortcut menu, you can use the arrow keys on the keyboard to navigate to the choice you want to make, and then press $\boxed{\text{Enter}}$.

$\boxed{\text{Ctrl}}$-$\boxed{\text{T}}$

Display the Windows taskbar

This shortcut lets you display the taskbar (for example, to access another application) without ending your slide show.

$\boxed{\text{F1}}$

Display the Slide Show Help dialog box

The Slide Show Help dialog box provides a quick reminder of the keyboard shortcuts available for controlling a presentation.

7

Outlook 2003 Keyboard Shortcuts

After Word, Outlook is perhaps the most text-based of the Office applications, so you might expect Outlook to offer plenty of keyboard shortcuts—and indeed it does. Outlook provides shortcuts for navigating among categories, creating new items (such as messages, contacts, and journal entries), applying formatting, and working with its main tools.

Notes on the Standard Shortcuts

Outlook supports the standard Office keyboard shortcuts discussed in "Shared Keyboard Shortcuts" in Chapter 3. The following exceptions are worth noting.

Shortcuts for Opening, Deleting, and Saving Items

Because Outlook doesn't work with files in the same way as the other Office applications, it uses a different method of opening items. Outlook also has a different shortcut for deleting the selected item.

`Ctrl`-`O`

Open the selected item

Select an item, and then press `Ctrl`-`O` to open it. You can press `Enter` instead to open some selected items.

`Ctrl`-`D`

Delete the selected item

You can also delete a selected item by pressing `Delete`.

`Ctrl`-`S`, `Shift`-`F12`

Save the file to the default Outlook folder

Shortcuts for Navigating from Pane to Pane

Use these shortcuts to navigate from pane to pane, and between the main Outlook window and the Folder List.

Tab, **F6**

Cycle among the Outlook window, the Navigation pane, and the Reading pane

Ctrl-**Shift**-**Tab**

Switch among the open windows or toolbars

Most of the time, pressing this shortcut switches focus from one window to another. But when a toolbar is selected, pressing **Ctrl**-**Shift**-**Tab** selects the next toolbar instead.

Shortcuts for Getting Around in the Navigation Pane

Outlook 2003 supports the following shortcuts for getting around in the Navigation pane. **Outlook XP, Outlook 2000 »** Outlook XP and Outlook 2000 do not have the Navigation pane, so they don't support these shortcuts.

Alt-**F1**

Toggle the display of the Navigation pane

←, **→**, **↑**, **↓**

Move the selection among the items in the Navigation pane

+ on the numeric keypad

Expand the selected group in the Navigation pane

− on the numeric keypad

Collapse the selected group in the Navigation pane

→

Expand a group in the message list

When working in the message list, you can use **→** to expand a group, as well as **+** on the numeric keypad.

←

Collapse a group in the message list

When working in the message list, you can use ⬅ to collapse a group, as well as
⊟ on the numeric keypad.

Going to Outlook Categories

Outlook offers Ctrl-*number* shortcuts for switching instantly to different categories
of items using the keyboard instead of the Go menu, the Navigation pane (in
Outlook 2003), or the Outlook bar (in Outlook XP and Outlook 2000).

Outlook XP, Outlook 2000 » Outlook XP and Outlook 2000 include neither the
Go menu (instead, they have a View | Go To submenu) nor most of these
shortcuts. Outlook XP and Outlook 2000 support the Ctrl-Y shortcut for going
to a folder, and the Ctrl-Shift-I shortcut for going to the Inbox.

Shortcuts for Going to Outlook Categories

Ctrl-1

Go to Mail

Ctrl-Shift-I

Go to the Inbox

Ctrl-Shift-O

Go to the Outbox

Ctrl-2

Go to Calendar

Ctrl-3

Go to Contacts

Ctrl-4

Go to Tasks

Ctrl-5

Go to Notes

Ctrl-6

Go to Folder List

Outlook 2003

Ctrl-7

Go to Shortcuts

Ctrl-8

Go to Journal

Ctrl-Y

Display the Go to Folder dialog box

The Go to Folder dialog box (shown here) lets you quickly navigate among the Outlook folders.

Ctrl-G

Display the Go To Date dialog box

Use the Go To Date dialog box to quickly navigate to a specific date. This shortcut works only in Calendar view when a date is selected.

When you have an item open (for example, an e-mail message or a Calendar item), you can use the following shortcuts to display the previous item or the next item.

Ctrl-.

Display the previous item

Ctrl-,

Display the next item

Creating New Items

In your work in Outlook, you'll often need to create new mail messages, posts, folders, and other items. Outlook offers shortcuts for these operations too.

Shortcuts for Creating New Items

Ctrl-N

Create a new mail message

Ctrl-Shift-S

Create a new post in the current folder

Ctrl-Shift-E

Create a new folder

When you press this shortcut, Outlook displays the Create New Folder dialog box (Figure 7-1). Enter the name for the folder, specify the type of item it will contain, and choose the folder in which to create it; then click the OK button.

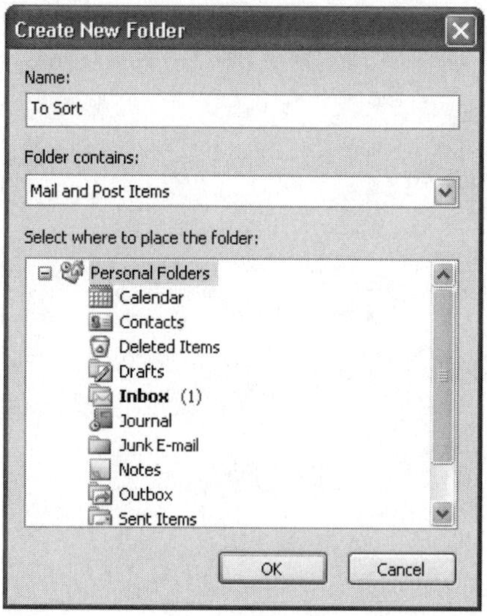

Figure 7-1

In the Create New Folder dialog box, enter the name for the new folder and specify its contents and the folder to create it in.

Outlook 2003

Ctrl-Shift-P

Create a new search folder

Outlook displays the New Search Folder dialog box (shown here) so that you can specify the details for the search folder. **Outlook XP, Outlook 2000 »** Outlook XP and Outlook 2000 don't use search folders.

Ctrl-Shift-A

Create a new appointment

Ctrl-Shift-C

Create a new contact

Ctrl-Shift-L

Create a new distribution list

Ctrl-Shift-K

Create a new task

Ctrl-Shift-U

Create a new task request

[Ctrl]-[Shift]-[J]

Create a new journal entry

[Ctrl]-[Shift]-[N]

Create a new note

[Ctrl]-[Shift]-[X]

Create a new fax

[Ctrl]-[Shift]-[H]

Display the New Office Document dialog box

In the New Office Document dialog box, choose which type of document to create—for example, a Microsoft Word Document or a Microsoft Excel Worksheet. Outlook activates or launches the corresponding application.

[Ctrl]-[Shift]-[Q]

Create a new meeting request

Working with Messages

If your job is halfway normal, you'll spend much of your time in Outlook working with messages: writing new messages and replies, forwarding messages to your more accommodating colleagues, filing messages in the hopes of reaching the bottom of your Inbox, and deleting virtual reams of spam. You can do all this from the keyboard.

Shortcuts for Working with Messages

[Ctrl]-[R]

Reply to the active message

[Ctrl]-[Shift]-[R]

Reply to all recipients of the active message

[Ctrl]-[F]

Forward the active message

Outlook 2003

Ctrl-Q

Mark the selected message as Read

Ctrl-U

Mark the selected message as Unread

Outlook XP, Outlook 2000 » The Ctrl-U shortcut doesn't work in Outlook XP and Outlook 2000. Instead, choose Edit | Mark as Unread.

F9

Send and receive all messages in all folders

Use this shortcut to send and check e-mail on all your accounts at once.

Shift-F9

Send and receive all messages in the current folder

Ctrl-Alt-M

Mark to download the selected messages

You can use this shortcut when you've configured your e-mail account to download headers only.

Ctrl-Alt-U

Unmark the selected headers

You can use this shortcut when you've configured your e-mail account to download headers only.

Alt-K, Ctrl-K

Check names

Ctrl-Shift-G

Flag the message for follow-up

Outlook displays the Flag for Follow Up dialog box (shown next) so that you can specify the type of follow-up flag to use.

Flag for Follow Up

Flagging marks an item to remind you that it needs to be followed up. After it has been followed up, you can mark it complete.

Flag to: Follow up   Flag color:

Due by: None   None

☐ Completed

Clear Flag   OK   Cancel

Ctrl-Alt-J

Mark the selected message as not junk

Select a message in your Junk folder and press this shortcut to rescue it.

Shift-F4

Find the next instance of the current search term

Use this keyboard shortcut when you're searching through an e-mail message.

Applying Formatting

Outlook supports some of the same keyboard shortcuts as Word for formatting text, even when you're not using Word as the e-mail editor.

Shortcuts for Applying Formatting

Ctrl-Shift-L

Apply bullets

Ctrl-T

Apply or increase the indent

Each press of this shortcut increases the indent by one tab stop.

Ctrl-Shift-T

Decrease the indent

Each press of this shortcut decreases the indent by one tab stop.

Ctrl-Spacebar, Ctrl-Shift-Z

Reset the formatting of the current paragraph or selection

Use this shortcut to quickly remove direct formatting that you've applied to text.

Outlook 2003

Accessing Key Tools

Outlook provides keyboard shortcuts for displaying the Send/Receive Groups dialog box, the Move Items dialog box and Copy Items dialog box, the Find bar, the Advanced Find dialog box, and the Address Book. Because you'll often need to access these tools, using keyboard shortcuts can save you time and effort.

Shortcuts for Accessing Key Tools

Ctrl-Alt-S

Display the Send/Receive Groups dialog box

Ctrl-Shift-Y

Display the Copy Items dialog box

Use the Copy Items dialog box to copy the selected item to another folder.

Outlook 2000 » The Ctrl-Shift-Y shortcut doesn't work in Outlook 2000. Instead, choose Edit | Copy to Folder to display the Copy Items dialog box.

Ctrl-Shift-V

Display the Move Items dialog box

Use the Move Items dialog box to move the selected item to another folder.

Ctrl-E, F3

Display the Find bar

Use the Find bar (shown here) to perform a basic Find operation. For more advanced searches, use the Advanced Find dialog box, shown next.

Outlook 2000 » The Ctrl-E shortcut doesn't work in Outlook 2000, and the Find bar's functionality is different. In Outlook 2000, pressing F3 displays the Advanced Find dialog box.

Look for: industrialized	▼ Search In ▼ Inbox	Find Now Clear	Options ▼ ✕

Ctrl-Shift-F

Display the Advanced Find dialog box

[Ctrl]-[Shift]-[B]

Display the Address Book

Working with Contacts

You can perform most operations with contacts easily from the keyboard instead of using the mouse. To select a contact, type the first few letters of the name to make Outlook select the entry. (If you have configured Outlook to display the last names first, type a few letters of the last name; if Outlook is displaying first names first, type a few letters of the first name.)

Shortcuts for Working with Contacts

[Home]

Select the first contact in the list

[End]

Select the last contact in the list

[↑]

Select the previous card

[↓]

Select the next card

[←]

Select the nearest card in the column to the left

[→]

Select the nearest card in the column to the right

[Ctrl]-[Spacebar]

Select or deselect the current card

[Shift]-[↓], [Ctrl]-[Shift]-[↓]

Extend the selection to the next card

[Shift]-[↑], [Ctrl]-[Shift]-[↑]

Extend the selection to the previous card

[Shift]-[Page Down]

Extend the selection to the last card on the last page

[Shift]-[Page Up]

Extend the selection to the first card on the first page

[Shift]-[Home]

Extend the selection to the first card in the list

[Shift]-[Home]

Extend the selection to the last card in the list

[Ctrl]-[Shift]-[D]

Display the New Call dialog box

F11

Select the Find a Contact box

Type the details of the contact you want to find in the Find a Contact box and press Enter to search.

Shortcuts for Navigating When a Contact Card Is Selected

You can use the following keyboard shortcuts when a contact card is selected.

Ctrl-↑

Move to the previous card

Ctrl-↓

Move to the next card

Ctrl-Home

Move to the first card in the list

Ctrl-End

Move to the last card in the list

Ctrl-Page Up

Move to the first card on the previous page

Ctrl-Page Down

Move to the first card on the next page

Ctrl-←

Move to the nearest card in the next column to the left

Ctrl-→

Move to the nearest card in the next column to the right

Outlook 2003

Shortcuts for Navigating When a Field on a Card Is Selected

When you've selected a field on a contact card, you can navigate by using the following keyboard shortcuts.

[Tab]

Move to the next field in the active card

If the current field is the last field in the active card, press [Tab] to move to the first field on the next card.

[Shift]-[Tab]

Move to the previous field in the active card

If the current field is the first field in the active card, press [Shift]-[Tab] to move to the last field on the previous card.

[Enter]

Move to the next field on the active card

If the current field has multiple lines, pressing [Enter] adds a line to the field.

[F2]

Switch the active field to Edit mode

[Enter]

Add a line to a multiline field

[Enter]

Move to the beginning of the line

[End]

Move to the end of the line

[↑]

Move to the previous line in a multiline field

[↓]

Move to the next line in a multiline field

Page Up

Move to the beginning of a multiline field

Page Down

Move to the end of a multiline field

Navigating in the Journal and in Tasks

The Journal and Tasks have their own shortcuts for navigating from item to item and for selecting items.

Shortcuts for Navigating in the Journal and in Tasks

←

Select the previous item

This shortcut works in the Journal, not in Tasks.

↑

Select the previous item

This shortcut works in Tasks, not in the Journal.

Shift-←, Shift-→

Add adjacent items to the selection

These shortcuts work in the Journal.

Ctrl-←-Spacebar, Ctrl-→-Spacebar

Add nonadjacent items to the selection

These shortcuts work in the Journal. Press Ctrl and the appropriate arrow key to move the selection outline to the item you want to add to the selection, and then press Spacebar to select the item. You can then manipulate all the selected items at once.

Enter

Open the selected items

This shortcut works in the Journal.

Page Up

Move up one screen

Page Down

Move down one screen

Home

Select the first item in the group or the first ungrouped item on the timeline

End

Select the last item in the group or the last ungrouped item on the timeline

Enter, →

Expand the selected group

Because Enter acts as a toggle for expanding and collapsing a group, most people find it easier than using → and ←.

Enter, ←

Collapse the selected group

Enter

Move the focus from the upper time scale to the lower time scale

When the focus is on the upper time scale, press Tab to move the focus to the lower time scale. When the focus is on the lower time scale, press Tab to move the focus to the first on-screen group or on-screen item.

Shift-Tab

Move the focus from the lower time scale to the upper time scale

Navigating in the Outlook Calendar

Like much of Outlook, the Calendar is largely graphical. But you can work in it effectively if you know the right keyboard shortcuts for navigation. The following sections present the shortcuts for general navigation in the Calendar, for navigating in Day view, Week view, and Month view, and for navigating in the Date Navigator.

Shortcuts for General Navigation in the Calendar

[Tab]

Select the next appointment

[Shift]-[Tab]

Select the previous appointment

[F6], [Ctrl]-[Tab]

Move among the Calendar, the TaskPad, and the Folder List

[Alt]-[1] to [Alt]-[9], [Alt]-[0]

Display one to nine days, or view ten days

Press [Alt] and the number of days you want to display. Press [Alt]-[0] (zero) for ten days.

[Alt]-[-]

Switch to Week view

[Alt]-[=]

Switch to Month view

[←]

Go to the previous day

[→]

Go to the next day

[Alt]-[↑]

Go to the same day in the previous week

[Alt]-[↓]

Go to the same day in the next week

Shortcuts for Navigating in Day View

[Home]

Select the time that begins the work day

This shortcut works only in Day view or Work Week view. In Week view, pressing [Home] selects the first day in the week.

You can specify the starting and ending times of the work day, and the days of the work week, in the Calendar Options dialog box. To display the Calendar Options dialog box, choose Tools | Options, and then click the Calendar Options button on the Preferences tab of the Options dialog box.

[End]

Select the time that ends the work day

[Page Up]

Go up one screenful

[Page Down]

Go down one screenful

[↑]

Select the previous block of time

[↓]

Select the next block of time

[Shift]-[↑]

Reduce the selected block of time, or select earlier blocks

[Shift]-[↓]

Increase the selected block of time, or reduce the existing selection

[Alt]-[↑]

Move the appointment to the same day in the previous week

Alt-↓

Move the appointment to the same day in the next week

Shortcuts for Navigating in Week View

Home

Go to the first day of the week

End

Go to the last day of the week

Page Up

Go to the same day of the week in the previous week

Page Down

Go to the same day of the week in the next week

Alt-↑

Move the appointment to an earlier time

Alt-↓

Move the appointment to a later time

Shortcuts for Navigating in Month View

You can use the following shortcuts to navigate in Month view in the Outlook Calendar. You'll notice that the Month view shortcuts have some overlap with Week view shortcuts.

Home

Go to the first day of the week

Press this shortcut to move the selection to the first day of the active week in the month. For example, if Wednesday the 21st is selected, pressing this shortcut moves the selection to Monday the 19th.

End

Go to the last day of the week

Press this shortcut to move the selection to the last day of the active week in the month.

Page Up

Go to the same day of the week five weeks earlier

Page Down

Go to the same day of the week five weeks later

Shortcuts for Navigating in Date Navigator

Alt - Home

Go to the first day of the current week

Alt - End

Go to the last day of the current week

Alt - ↑

Go to the same day in the previous week

Alt - ↓

Go to the same day in the next week

Alt - Page Up

Go to the first day of the month

Alt - Page Down

Go to the last day of the month

Access Keyboard Shortcuts

Access provides a large number of keyboard shortcuts for working in its various different features. Many of Access's features use either standard Windows and Office shortcuts or slight variations on them, so you'll probably notice some overlap in the different sections of this chapter. You'll also notice some subtle differences between the same shortcuts in different contexts, so be careful when you use them.

Notes on the Standard Shortcuts

Access supports the standard Office keyboard shortcuts discussed in "Shared Keyboard Shortcuts" in Chapter 3. The following exceptions are worth noting.

Shortcuts for Minimizing and Navigating Among Windows

Access lets you open only one database at once, but you can have many windows on that database open at the same time. Access keeps all the open database windows inside the same application window. When you minimize a database window, it's minimized within the Access window rather than minimized to a separate button on the Windows taskbar. Access provides shortcuts for navigating among minimized windows.

F11

Bring the database window to the front

Access 2000 » In Access 2000, you can also press Alt-F1 to bring the database window to the front.

Ctrl-F6

Select the next database window

Ctrl - Shift - F6

Select the previous database window

Enter

Restore the selected minimized window

This shortcut works only when all the windows are minimized.

Ctrl - F10 , then Enter

Restore or maximize the selected minimized window

Use Ctrl F6 or Ctrl - Shift - F6 to select a window using the keyboard so that you can restore or maximize it using either of these shortcuts.

Shortcuts for Saving Databases and Creating New Databases

Access has slight differences in the shortcuts for saving databases and creating new databases.

F12 , Alt - F12

Display the Save As dialog box

You can use Alt - F2 instead of the standard F12 to display the Save As dialog box for saving the active object under a different name, in a different location, or both.

Ctrl - N

Create a new database

Access 2003 and Access XP display the New File task pane so that you can choose the type of database to create. **Access 2000 »** Access 2000 displays the New dialog box.

Shortcuts for Finding and Replacing Items

Access also has some differences in the shortcuts for finding and replacing items.

Ctrl - F

Display the Find tab of the Find and Replace dialog box

This shortcut works only in Datasheet view and Form view.

[Ctrl]-[H]

Display the Replace tab of the Find and Replace dialog box

This shortcut works only in Datasheet view and Form view.

[Shift]-[F4]

Find the next instance of the search text

This shortcut works only in Datasheet view and Form view.

Shortcuts for Editing Text and Data

Access supports most standard Office shortcuts for editing text. For example, you can use [←], [→], [↑], and [↓] to navigate through text, press [Ctrl]-[C] to copy the selection, and press [Ctrl]-[V] to paste an item from the Clipboard. The main constraint is that you need to press [F2] to make a field editable. You can tell easily enough if you need to press [F2]: press it if the selected field isn't displaying the insertion point.

[Home]

Move the insertion point to the beginning of a single-line field

[End]

Move the insertion point to the end of a single-line field

[Ctrl]-[Home]

Move the insertion point to the beginning of a multiline field

[Ctrl]-[End]

Move the insertion point to the end of a multiline field

[Ctrl]-[Delete]

Delete all characters from the insertion point to the end of the field

[Esc]

Undo changes in the current field or current record

Press [Esc] once to undo changes in the current field, and again to undo changes in the current record.

Access

Basic Navigation in Access

This section discusses the keyboard shortcuts that you can use for navigating in most objects in Access. Beyond these common keyboard shortcuts, most objects support shortcuts of their own; you'll meet these shortcuts later in this chapter.

Shortcuts for Navigation

⬇

Move down one line

⬆

Move up one line

Page Down

Move down one page

Page Up

Move up one page

Shortcuts for Recalculating and Refreshing Data

You can use the following shortcuts widely in Access to recalculate fields, refresh a Lookup field or drop-down list, or requery a data source.

F9

Recalculate the fields in the window, or refresh a Lookup field or drop-down list

Shift - F9

Requery the data source to update records

Press this shortcut to rerun the current query for the active form or datasheet.

Shortcuts for Taking Widely Used Actions

You can use the following keyboard shortcuts to perform widely used actions in Access.

F2

Display the full URL for the selected hyperlink

$\boxed{\text{Shift}}\text{-}\boxed{\text{F2}}$

> *Display the Zoom dialog box*

Use the Zoom dialog box to enter text more easily when working in a small input area.

$\boxed{\text{Ctrl}}\text{-}\boxed{.},\ \boxed{\text{Ctrl}}\text{-}\boxed{\rightarrow}$

> *Move forward to the next available view*

This shortcut works in items such as tables, forms, queries, reports, pages, PivotTable lists, PivotChart reports, and Access projects. The views available depend on the item.

$\boxed{\text{Ctrl}}\text{-}\boxed{.},\ \boxed{\text{Ctrl}}\text{-}\boxed{\leftarrow}$

> *Move backward to the next available view*

This shortcut works in items such as tables, forms, queries, reports, pages, PivotTable lists, PivotChart reports, and Access projects. The views available depend on the item.

Navigating in the Objects Bar and Object List

The Objects bar and Object list enable you to move quickly from one item to another in Access.

Shortcuts for Navigating in the Objects Bar and Object List

$\boxed{\text{Ctrl}}\text{-}\boxed{\text{Tab}}$

> *Select the next item in the Objects bar*

$\boxed{\text{Ctrl}}\text{-}\boxed{\text{Shift}}\text{-}\boxed{\text{Tab}}$

> *Select the previous item in the Objects bar*

$\boxed{\uparrow}$

> *Move the selection up one line*

$\boxed{\downarrow}$

> *Move the selection down one line*

[Page Up]

Move the selection up one window

[Page Down]

Move the selection down one window

[Home]

Move to the first object in the list

[End]

Move to the last object in the list

[Enter]

Open or run the selected object

The effect of pressing [Enter] depends on the type of object you've selected. Pressing [Enter]:

- Opens a table or query in Datasheet view

- Opens a form in Form view

- Opens a report in Print Preview

- Opens a data access page in Page view

- Runs a macro

[Alt]-[O]

Open the selected object

This shortcut opens a table or query in Datasheet view, and opens a form in Form view.

[Alt]-[N]

Create a new object of the selected type

Select the category of object in the Objects bar, and then press [Alt]-[N] to start creating a new object of that type. For example, select Reports in the Objects bar, and press [Alt]-[N] to display the New Report dialog box for creating a new report.

[Ctrl]-[Enter], [Alt]-[D]

Open the selected object in Design view

These shortcuts work for tables, forms, queries, reports, data access pages, macros, and modules.

Working in Design View

The following sections discuss the keyboard shortcuts that Access provides for navigating in Design view and for editing, moving, and resizing controls.

Shortcuts for Navigating in Design View

[F2]

Toggle between Navigation mode and Edit mode

In Navigation mode, you can move the selection from field to field by using the arrow keys. In Edit mode, Access displays an insertion point, and the arrow keys move the insertion point from character to character in the field.

[F4], [Alt]-[Enter]

Display the property sheet

This shortcut works for forms and reports in Design view, and for Access projects. Once you've selected a tab, you can move from tab to tab in the property sheet by pressing [→] (to display the next tab) or [←] (to display the previous tab).
Access 2000 » The [F4] shortcut to display the property sheet doesn't work in Access 2000. Use [Alt]-[Enter] instead.

[F5]

Switch a form from Design view to Form view

[F6]

Switch between the upper part and lower part of a window

This shortcut works in Design view for tables, macros, and queries, and in the Advanced Filter/Sort window.

[F7]

Switch to the Code Builder from Design view

Use this shortcut from Design view for a form or a report.

Access 2000 » The [F7] shortcut doesn't work in Access 2000.

Access

Shift - F7

Switch to Design view from the Visual Basic Editor

Use this shortcut from Design view for a form or report. If a control's property sheet is selected in Design view for a form or report, pressing this shortcut moves the focus to the design surface. **Access 2000 »** The Shift - F7 shortcut doesn't work in Access 2000.

F8

Display the field list in a form, a report, or a data access page

If the field list is already displayed, pressing F8 selects the field list.

Shortcuts for Editing Controls in Design View

You can use the following keyboard shortcuts to edit controls in Design view for forms and reports. Access provides shortcuts for moving the control either along the page's grid (which is useful for aligning controls with minimal effort) or independently of the page's grid.

Shift - Enter

Add a control to the active section

Use this shortcut when accessing the field list in a form, a report, or a data access page.

←

Move the selected control left one pixel along the page's grid

Ctrl - ←

Move the selected control left one pixel, ignoring the grid

→

Move the selected control right one pixel along the page's grid

Ctrl - →

Move the selected control right one pixel, ignoring the grid

↑

Move the selected control up one pixel along the page's grid

⌈Ctrl⌉-⌈↑⌉

Move the selected control up one pixel, ignoring the grid

⌈↓⌉

Move the selected control down one pixel along the page's grid

⌈Ctrl⌉-⌈↓⌉

Move the selected control down one pixel, ignoring the page's grid

⌈Shift⌉-⌈←⌉

Decrease the width of the selected control by one pixel

⌈Shift⌉-⌈→⌉

Increase the width of the selected control by one pixel

⌈Shift⌉-⌈↑⌉

Decrease the height of the selected control by one pixel

⌈Shift⌉-⌈↓⌉

Increase the height of the selected control by one pixel

Working with Text and Data

Access supports standard keyboard shortcuts for selecting text when you're working within a field. For example, press ⌈Shift⌉-⌈→⌉ to extend the selection one character to the right, or press ⌈Shift⌉-⌈←⌉ to reduce the selection one character to the left.

Shortcuts for Selecting Fields and Records

You can use the following keyboard shortcuts to select fields and records.

⌈Tab⌉

Select the next field

⌈Shift⌉-⌈Spacebar⌉

Toggle between selecting a record and selecting the first field of the record
This shortcut works in Navigation mode.

Access

Shift-↑

Extend the selection from the current record to the previous record

This shortcut works when the current record is selected.

Shift-↓

Extend the selection from the current record to the next record

This shortcut works when the current record is selected.

Ctrl-A, Ctrl-Shift-Spacebar

Select all the records

Shortcuts for Extending the Selection

You can use the following keyboard shortcuts to extend the selection.

F8

Turn on Extend mode and extend the selection

In Extend mode, Access displays EXT in the lower-left corner of the window. Once you've toggled Extend mode on, you can extend the selection by pressing F8 again. The second press selects the word, the third press selects the field, the fourth press selects the record (in Datasheet view), and the next keypress (the fifth in Datasheet view, the fourth in other views) selects all records.

→

Extend the selection to the field to the right in the same row

This shortcut works only in Datasheet view after you've pressed F8 to turn on Extend mode.

←

Extend the selection to the field to the left in the same row

This shortcut works only in Datasheet view after you've pressed F8 to turn on Extend mode.

↑

Extend the selection to the previous row

This shortcut works only in Datasheet view after you've selected an entire cell or row and pressed F8 to turn on Extend mode.

[↓]

Extend the selection to the next row

This shortcut works only in Datasheet view after you've selected an entire cell or row and pressed [F8] to turn on Extend mode.

[Shift]-[F8]

Undo the previous extension

Press [Shift]-[F8] to reduce the selection by the last press of [F8].

[Esc]

Turn off Extend mode

Press [Esc] after you've finished selecting the relevant items in Extend mode.

[Ctrl]-[Spacebar]

Toggle selection of the active column

Press this shortcut to select the active column (if it's not selected) or to deselect it (if it is selected). This shortcut works only when you've selected an entire cell (not just part of a cell).

[Shift]-[→]

Extend the selection to the column to the right

For this shortcut to work, the active column must already be selected. (Use the previous shortcut to select it if necessary.)

[Shift]-[←]

Extend the selection to the column to the left

For this shortcut to work, the active column must already be selected. (Use the previous shortcut to select it if necessary.)

Shortcuts for Moving Columns in Datasheet View

You can use the following keyboard shortcuts to move columns in Datasheet view.

[Ctrl]-[Shift]-[F8]

Switch on Move mode

In Move mode, you can use [←] and [→] to move the selected column or columns.

Access

⏴

Move the selected columns to the left in Move mode

⏵

Move the selected columns to the right in Move mode

Shortcuts for Entering Data in Datasheet View or Form View

You can use the following keyboard shortcuts to enter data quickly in Datasheet view or Form view.

Ctrl-;

Insert the current date in the default format

Ctrl-Shift-:

Insert the current time in the default format

Ctrl-Alt-Spacebar

Insert the default value for the active field

Ctrl-'

Copy the value from the same field in the previous record

Ctrl-Shift-+

Add a new record to the database

Ctrl--

Delete the active record

Shift-Enter

Save changes to the active record

Ctrl-Enter

Insert a line in a multiline field

Navigating in Datasheet View and Form View

The first section here discusses the keyboard shortcuts that Datasheet view and Form view share for navigation. The following sections cover the shortcuts that work differently in Datasheet view and in Form view.

Shortcuts for Both Datasheet View and Form View

[F5]

Select the Record Number box on the status bar

Type the record number in the Record Number box and press [Enter] to access that record.

[Tab], [→]

Select the next field

[Shift]-[Tab], [←]

Select the previous field

[↓]

Select the next field

[↑]

Select the previous field

[Home]

Select the first field in the active record

[End]

Select the last field in the active record

[Ctrl]-[↓]

Select the current field in the last record

[Ctrl]-[↑]

Select the current field in the first record

Access

Ctrl - End

Select the last field in the last record

Ctrl - Home

Select the first field in the first record

Shortcuts for Navigating in Datasheet View

Apart from the shortcuts common to Datasheet view and Form view discussed in the previous section, you can use the following keyboard shortcuts to navigate in Datasheet view.

Page Down

Display the next screen of data downward

Page Up

Display the next screen of data upward

Ctrl - Page Down

Display the next screen of data to the right

Ctrl - Page Up

Display the next screen of data to the left

Shortcuts for Navigating in Form View

Apart from the shortcuts common to Datasheet view and Form view discussed earlier, you can use the following shortcuts for navigating in forms that contain more than one page.

Page Down

Display the next page

Pressing Page Down at the end of the record displays the same page of the next record.

Page Up

Display the previous page

Pressing Page Up at the end of the record displays the same page of the previous record.

Shortcuts for Navigating Between the Main Form and a Subform

[Tab]

Move from the preceding field in the main form to the subform

[Shift]-[Tab]

Move from the following field in the main form to the subform

[Ctrl]-[Tab]

Move from the subform to the next field in the main form

If the main form contains no fields after the subform, pressing [Ctrl]-[Tab] selects the first field in the next record.

[Ctrl]-[Shift]-[Tab]

Move from the subform to the previous field in the main form

If the main form contains no fields before the subform, pressing [Ctrl]-[Shift]-[Tab] selects the last field in the previous record.

Shortcuts for Working with Subdatasheets

[Ctrl]-[Shift]-[↓]

Expand the subdatasheet

[Ctrl]-[Shift]-[↑]

Collapse the subdatasheet

[Tab]

Move from the last field of the previous record to the subdatasheet

You can also press [Tab] to move from the last field of the subdatasheet to the next field in the datasheet.

[Shift]-[Tab]

Move from the first field of the following record to the subdatasheet

[Ctrl]-[Tab]

Move from the subdatasheet to the first field of the next record

Access

[Ctrl]-[Shift]-[Tab]

Move from the subdatasheet to the last field of the previous record

>> Note: *If you don't want to access the subdatasheet, press* [↓] *to move past it downward or* [↑] *to move past it upward.*

Navigating in Print Preview

Print Preview may seem a natural candidate for using the mouse, but you can navigate it faster and more effectively by using keyboard shortcuts—if you know the right ones.

Shortcuts for Navigating in Print Preview

[F5]

Select the page number box

Type the page number and press [Enter] to display the page.

[Page Down], [↓]

Display the next page

These shortcuts work only when the Fit to Window option is turned on.

[Page Up], [↑]

Display the previous page

These shortcuts work only when the Fit to Window option is turned on.

[←], [→], [↑], [↓]

Scroll in small increments

Press the appropriate arrow key for the direction you want to scroll in. These shortcuts work only if Fit to Window is *not* turned on.

[Ctrl]-[↓]

Scroll to the bottom of the page

[Ctrl]-[↑]

Scroll to the top of the page

Ctrl-→, End

> *Scroll to the right side of the page*

Ctrl-←, Home

> *Scroll to the left side of the page*

Ctrl-Home

> *Scroll to the upper-left corner of the page*

Ctrl-End

> *Scroll to the lower-right corner of the page*

Navigating in the Database Diagram Window in a Project

Access provides keyboard shortcuts for moving from table to table, from cell to cell, and from a table's title bar to a cell in the Database Diagram window.

Shortcuts for Navigating in the Database Diagram Window

Esc

> *Move to the table's title bar from a cell*

Enter

> *Move back to the last cell edited from the table's title bar*

Enter

> *Move among table title bars, or move among cells*
>
> When a table title bar is selected, press Tab to select the next table title bar. When a cell is selected, press Tab to select the next cell.

Page Down

> *Display the next page of the table or diagram*

Page Up

> *Display the previous page of the table or diagram*

Access

Working in the Grid Pane

Access provides keyboard shortcuts for moving quickly about the grid pane, toggling between Edit mode and Navigation mode, and toggling between Insert mode and Overstrike mode when you're editing in a cell.

Shortcuts for Working in the Grid Pane

F2

Toggle between Edit mode and Navigation mode

Insert

Toggle between Insert mode and Overstrike mode

This shortcut works only when you're editing in a cell.

>> **Note:** *When you're not editing a cell, press* Insert *to insert a row between existing rows.*

Ctrl-↓

Select the last cell in the active column

Ctrl-↑

Select the first cell in the active column

Ctrl-Home

Select the top-left cell in the visible part of the grid

Ctrl-End

Select the bottom-right cell in the visible part of the grid

Working in PivotTable View

Access provides a wealth of keyboard shortcuts for working in PivotTable view. The following sections present these keyboard shortcuts broken up by category, starting with the basic keyboard shortcuts for operations such as moving the selection and selecting cells.

Basic Shortcuts for PivotTable View

[Tab]

Select the next element to the right or down

Pressing [Tab] moves the selection from left to right, and then down.

[Shift]-[Tab]

Select the next element to the left or up

Pressing [Shift]-[Tab] moves the selection to the left. When the selection is in the leftmost cell, pressing [Shift]-[Tab] selects the last cell in the previous row.

[Enter]

Select the next element down or to the right

Pressing [Enter] moves the selection down, and then to the right.

[Shift]-[Enter]

Select the next element up

Pressing [Shift]-[Enter] moves the selection to the cell above the active cell. If the active cell is the topmost cell, pressing [Shift]-[Enter] selects the last cell in the previous column.

[Ctrl]-[Enter]

Select the detail cells for the next item in the row area

[Ctrl]-[Shift]-[Enter]

Select the detail cells for the previous item in the row area

[Shift]-[←], [Shift]-[→], [Shift]-[↑], [Shift]-[↓]

Extend or reduce the selection

Press the appropriate arrow key to extend or reduce the current selection.

[Ctrl]-[←], [Ctrl]-[→], [Ctrl]-[↑], [Ctrl]-[↓]

Move the selection to the last cell

Press the appropriate arrow key for the direction of the last cell you want to select.

[Alt]-[Shift]-[←], [Alt]-[Shift]-[→], [Alt]-[Shift]-[↑], [Alt]-[Shift]-[↓]

Move the selected item

Press the appropriate arrow key for the direction you want to move the selected item.

[Home]

Select the first cell in the active row

[End]

Select the last cell in the active row

[Ctrl]-[Home]

Select the first cell in the first row

[Ctrl]-[End]

Select the last cell in the last row

[Ctrl]-[Shift]-[Home]

Extend the selection to the first cell in the first row

[Ctrl]-[Shift]-[End]

Extend the selection to the last cell in the last row

[Ctrl]-[Spacebar]

Select the field for the active data, total, or detail item

[Shift]-[Spacebar]

Select the row containing the active cell

[Ctrl]-[A]

Select the whole PivotTable view

[Page Down]

Display the next screen

[Page Up]

Display the previous screen

[Shift]-[Page Down]

Extend the selection by one screen down

[Shift]-[Page Up]

Reduce the selection by one screen

[Alt]-[Page Down]

Display the next screen to the right

[Alt]-[Page Up]

Display the next screen to the left

[Alt]-[Shift]-[Page Down]

Extend the selection by one page to the right

[Alt]-[Shift]-[Page Up]

Extend the selection by one page to the left

[Ctrl]-[E]

Export the contents of the PivotTable to Excel

Shortcuts for Displaying, Hiding, Sorting, and Filtering Data

You can use the following keyboard shortcuts to filter data in PivotTable view.

[Ctrl]-[8]

Toggle the display of the expand indicators beside items

[Ctrl]-[=]

Expand the selected item

[Ctrl]-[-]

Hide the current item

Ctrl-T

Toggle AutoFilter on and off

Ctrl-Shift-A

Sort the selected field's data in ascending order

Ascending order sorts from A to Z and from 0 (zero) to 9.

Ctrl-Shift-Z

Sort the selected field's data in descending order

Descending order sorts from Z to A and from 9 to 0 (zero).

Alt-Shift-↑

Move the selected item up

Alt-Shift-←

Move the selected item to the left

Alt-Shift-↓

Move the selected item down

Alt-Shift-→

Move the selected item to the right

Shortcuts for Working with the Field List

You can use the following keyboard shortcuts for working with the field list in a PivotTable.

Ctrl-L

Display or activate the field list

Shift-↑

Move to the previous item, adding it to the current selection

Ctrl-↑

Move to the previous item without adding it to the current selection

[Shift]-[↓]

> *Move to the next item, adding it to the current selection*

[Ctrl]-[↓]

> *Move to the next item without adding it to the current selection*

[Ctrl]-[Spacebar]

> *Toggle the selection of the item*
>
> If the item is selected, pressing [Ctrl]-[Spacebar] deselects it; if the item isn't selected, pressing [Ctrl]-[Spacebar] selects it.

[+] on the numeric keypad

> *Expand the current item in the field list*

[-] on the numeric keypad

> *Collapse the current item in the field list*

[Alt]-[F4]

> *Close the field list*

Shortcuts for Adding Fields and Totals in a PivotTable

Access provides keyboard shortcuts for adding fields and totals in a PivotTable using a variety of different summary functions.

[Ctrl]-[Shift]-[S]

> *Add a new Sum total field to the selected field*

[Ctrl]-[Shift]-[C]

> *Add a new Count total field for the selected field*

[Ctrl]-[Shift]-[M]

> *Add a new Min total field for the selected field*

[Ctrl]-[Shift]-[X]

> *Add a new Max total field for the selected field*

Access

Ctrl-Shift-E

Add a new Average total field for the selected field

Ctrl-Shift-D

Add a new Standard Deviation total field for the selected field

Ctrl-Shift-T

Add a new Standard Deviation Population total field for the selected field

Ctrl-Shift-V

Add a new Variance total field for the selected field

Ctrl-Shift-R

Add a new Variance Population total field for the selected field

Ctrl-Shift-B

Toggle subtotals and grand totals on and off for the selected field

Ctrl-F

Add a calculated detail field

Shortcuts for Changing the Layout of a PivotTable

You can use the following keyboard shortcuts to change the layout of a PivotTable.

Ctrl-1 on the key row

Move the selected field to the row area

Ctrl-2 on the key row

Move the selected field to the column area

Ctrl-3 on the key row

Move the selected field to the filter area

Ctrl-4 on the key row

Move the selected field to the detail area

`Ctrl`-`←`

Move the selected field to a higher level

`Ctrl`-`→`

Move the selected field to a lower level

Shortcuts for Changing the Number Format of a Field

Access provides the following seven keyboard shortcuts for changing the number format of the selected field.

`Ctrl`-`Shift`-`~`

Apply the general number format

`Ctrl`-`Shift`-`$`

Apply the currency format

The currency format has two decimal places and uses parentheses around negative numbers.

`Ctrl`-`Shift`-`%`

Apply the percentage format with no decimal places

`Ctrl`-`Shift`-`^`

Apply the exponential number format with two decimal places

`Ctrl`-`Shift`-`#`

Apply the date format with day, month, and year

`Ctrl`-`Shift`-`@`

Apply the time format with hour, minute, and am/pm

`Ctrl`-`Shift`-`!`

Apply the numeric format with two decimal places

This numeric format uses the thousands separator and a minus sign for negative values.

Working in a PivotChart

You can use the arrow keys to select items and groups of items in a PivotChart.

Shortcuts for Working in a PivotChart

[→]

Select the next item

[←]

Select the previous item

[↓]

Select the next group of items

[↑]

Select the previous group of items

Choosing a Better Keyboard

Every Windows computer comes with a keyboard and either a mouse or some other form of pointing device, such as a touchpad or pointing stick. The keyboard is usually a basic device that fulfills little more than the minimal requirements of having the right number of keys arranged in a conventional fashion and having a suitable connection to the computer, such as a PS/2 plug, a USB plug, or a wireless connection.

If what's sitting on your desk and keeping your fingertips blunt is a basic keyboard, you're likely to benefit from an upgrade. This appendix discusses what kinds of keyboards are available and how to choose a suitable keyboard for your needs. (For help on configuring your keyboard and choosing such accessibility options as will help you, see Chapter 1.)

Considerations for Choosing a Keyboard

At the risk of generalizing horribly, keyboards fall into three categories: conventional, serious, and specialized (or strange) keyboards. The following sections discuss these categories.

First, though, here are general considerations to keep in mind when choosing a new keyboard:

- You must choose the keyboard yourself, because only you can tell whether it suits you. One person's dream ergonomic keyboard is another person's carpal tunnel of horrors.

- Try to type for several minutes on any keyboard you're considering buying so that you can get a fair idea of its strong points and weak points.

- Generally speaking, the more expensive a keyboard is, the higher its build quality should be. But if all you need is a conventional keyboard, you should be able to find a decent one without spending a lot of money. Besides, expense doesn't necessarily bear any relation to comfort.

- If you're likely to spill coffee, soda, or water on your keyboard, or shower it with crumbs, you may prefer to stick with a cheaper keyboard so that it costs less to replace. Alternatively, make sure that a keyboard *skin* (a cover through which you use the keyboard) is available for the model you plan to buy, or find a company that can manufacture custom skins for any keyboard.

- You don't need to be suffering from carpal tunnel or RSI syndrome before you start using an ergonomic keyboard, although sadly for many people this is the normal progression. If you spend several hours or more each day typing, seriously consider an ergonomic keyboard. You should also take such steps as possible to reduce the amount of typing you do—for example, by using keyboard shortcuts, macros, and features built into your software (such as AutoCorrect or glossary features).

Here are more specific criteria to ask yourself when you lay hands on the keyboard. They're largely obvious, but you'll kick yourself if you skip them.

- Does it have all the keys you want?

- Are the keys arranged where you need them to be?

- Are the keys the right size? Standard key spacing is 19 mm from the middle of one key to the middle of the next key.

- Is the key travel adequate? Key travel of 3 mm is about standard. Many laptop keyboards necessarily have less travel.

- Do you like the "feel" of the keyboard? This is almost entirely subjective: some people like keyboards with a firm feel; others prefer a soft feel; some like a firm response and audible click when a key is pressed, others a subtler response and no audible click.

- Does it have the right type of connector for the computer or computers you want to use it with? These days, most computers use PS/2 connectors—the kind with a small round connector at the end—rather than the 5-pin DIN connector (a larger round connector) used on older keyboards. Some "legacy-lite" or "legacy-free" computers require USB keyboards. You can get various kinds of keyboard connectors if necessary, but they all cost money and clutter your computing area.

- Is the keyboard the color you want? Computer beige is the most widely used color for keyboards, but many black keyboards are available too. Beyond these colors (or noncolors), your choices are limited. The next most popular "color" after beige and black is perhaps aluminum, with several aluminum keyboards available.

All of these issues are easy enough to resolve if you can try the keyboard before you buy it. If you must buy without trying, make sure you can return the keyboard if it doesn't suit you.

Why Wireless Keyboards Can Threaten Your Privacy

If you don't especially appreciate having your keyboard tethered to your PC by a six-foot cable, you may be drawn by the attractions of wireless keyboards, which let you move the keyboard freely about in a room's distance or so of your computer. But before you invest in a wireless keyboard, be clear on possible problems that they can bring with them.

The main problem is that a wireless keyboard can transmit signals to other wireless receivers in the neighborhood as well as to your receiver. In one documented instance in Stavanger, Norway, the user of a wireless keyboard found that his computer was receiving signals transmitted from another wireless keyboard. From the contents, he learned that the other wireless keyboard was 150 meters (500 feet) and several walls removed from his computer.

The second, and secondary, problem is that you typically won't know if your wireless keyboard is transmitting what you type to another computer as well as to your own. Unless your keystrokes fail to show up on your computer, there's no reason for you to suspect a problem until you receive the unwelcome news from a neighbor.

Most large computer stores carry a variety of keyboards and make the most popular (or most promoted) models available for customers to try. While large stores typically have some of the more widely used ergonomic keyboards, if you need a specialized model, you'll probably do better to visit a specialized computer-ergonomics store.

Conventional Keyboards

Conventional PC keyboards are like those layouts you saw in Chapter 1. Conventional desktop keyboards contain 101 or more keys (many have 104 or 105 keys), while conventional laptop keyboards contain around 85 keys, with some of those keys performing additional functions via modifier keys (typically the Function key). Some wide-screen laptops are large enough to include full keyboards of 101 keys or more.

Serious Keyboards

The next category of keyboards is best classed as "serious"—keyboards that are more or less conventional in shape and layout but are designed for heavy-duty work.

If you find that conventional keyboards are too flimsy or have too light a feel, consider what enthusiasts call a *battleship board*—a heavy-duty keyboard that includes much more metal and correspondingly less plastic than lower-priced keyboards. The main difference between battleship boards and regular keyboards is that battleship boards usually use a buckling-spring switch under each key, whereas regular keyboards use switches constructed around rubber domes of one sort or another. Buckling springs give a much more solid click (both tactile and aural) than rubber domes and feel much more solid. They're also heavier in weight, heavier duty, and more expensive.

This essential difference distinguishes most battleship boards from regular keyboards, but you'll also find other serious keyboards that don't use buckling-spring switches on the keys. Some of these serious keyboards have different layouts than standard keyboards. For example, some serious keyboards have the function keys on the left side of the keyboard instead of on the top row. Some even have two sets of function keys: one on the left side, one on the top row. Few people need such a different layout of function keys, but you'll know if you do.

IBM used to make the best battleship boards, and their technology lives on. Perhaps the best site for battleship boards of one type or another is PCKeyboard.com (**www.pckeyboard.com**). They are a division of Unicomp, which bought keyboard technology from Lexmark International, the company that used to make the keyboards for IBM after being spun off from IBM itself.

Specialized Keyboards

The last category of keyboards is specialized keyboards. Some people prefer to call them *strange* keyboards—and some of them are indeed strange. But if your work (or play) involves a lot of typing, a specialized keyboard can save you plenty of time, effort, and grief.

Dividing specialized keyboards into categories tends to be difficult, because there are many different types of keyboards. But here's a stab at division:

- Undersized and oversized keyboards
- Keyboards with integrated pointing devices
- Split keyboards
- Split and tilted keyboards
- Superergonomic keyboards
- One-handed keyboards

If you're in the market for a specialized keyboard, you may find that the essential division is between keyboards that use a modified version of the standard keyboard layout and keyboards that use a radically different layout. Keyboards that use a modified version of a standard layout are usually easy to get started with, because you don't have to learn entirely new typing habits. Keyboards that use radically different layouts can offer greater ergonomic benefits or ease of use, but you'll have to learn to type on them, which can involve a considerable learning curve.

If you use the same keyboard for all your data entry, learning a new keyboard layout may be sensible and easy. If you need to use various computers, you'll probably be better off using a specialized keyboard that modifies the standard keyboard layout.

Specialized keyboards start at several hundred dollars and progress to more than a thousand, making them a serious investment. But if you're starting to suffer from RSI—or attempting to avoid it altogether—the investment may well make sense.

Undersized and Oversized Keyboards

The first type of specialized keyboard you may want is an undersized or oversized keyboard. Generally speaking, there are two types of undersized keyboards: space-saving keyboards designed for small working surfaces, and keyboards with smaller-than-usual keys for people with small hands. If you look hard enough, you can find space-saving keyboards that use smaller-than-usual keys as well.

If your desk or other working surface is short of space, a compact keyboard may be the answer. Some compact keyboards have no numeric keypad, while others have an embedded numeric keypad like those many notebooks have. If space is at a premium, consider a compact keyboard that has an integrated pointing device, such as a pointing stick, a trackball, or a touchpad. Because the pointing stick is usually located among the keys rather than requiring an area of its own, keyboards with pointing sticks tend to be the most compact solution available.

As you learned earlier in this appendix, standard key spacing for a keyboard is 19 mm from the middle of one key to the middle of the next key. If you've learned to type on a keyboard with this key spacing, and your hands aren't extra small or extra large, you'll probably find it comfortable enough. But if your hands *are* extra small, you may be better off with a keyboard that has smaller-than-usual key spacing. A couple of millimeters makes a considerable difference: 17 mm spacing (which you'll find on various ultraportable laptops) is manageable for most people, but 16 mm feels very cramped. At 15 mm and smaller sizes, anyone with normal-size fingertips has to type very accurately so as not to strike one or more neighboring keys by mistake. (If you've ever handled one of the Toshiba Libretto micro-notebooks, that's 15 mm keyboard spacing.)

Undersized keyboards are relatively easy to find if you search on the Web; so are oversized keyboards—at least, keyboards with hugely oversized keys, not the fractionally larger keys (say, 20 mm or 21 mm spacing) that people with large hands might find useful. A typical oversized keyboard, such as the Big Keys Keyboard (available from various sources), has keys that are one-inch square, which is four times the size of standard keys on a typical desktop keyboard. Keys this large aren't much good for touch-typing unless you have giant hands, but they're great for industrial environments (gloved fingers) and for mild disabilities (a bigger key is easier to strike without blipping another key). Large keys can also be good for children, because the letters are easier to spot; and some models come with the keys in a variety of colors.

Keyboards with Integrated Pointing Devices

As you read in the previous section, some undersized keyboards include integrated pointing devices. Some full-size keyboards have them as well. Most of these pointing devices are pointing sticks, touchpads, or miniature trackballs, but if you search, you can also find keyboards with more esoteric pointing devices.

Some of the stranger keyboard types include advanced pointing devices. For example, the TouchStream keyboards from FingerWorks (**www.fingerworks.com**) include a custom pointing device that interprets the gestures from your hands.

Split Keyboards

Standard keyboards have been blamed for causing carpal tunnel syndrome by forcing users to hold their hands (or even wrists) parallel to each other. In fact, this supposed compulsion is largely imaginary: it's actually easier to type with your hands pointing inwards at a natural angle even on a regular keyboard.

Even so, many users find split keyboards more comfortable than regular keyboards. In a split keyboard layout, the keys assigned to the right hand are physically separated from the keys assigned to the left hand, often by several inches, to provide easier positions for the hands and arms.

If you learned to type with the correct fingers, you should have no problems with the division of the keyboard. If you learned "bad" habits such as reaching over for B with your right forefinger, you'll need to unlearn such habits before you can use a split keyboard easily.

The Microsoft Natural Keyboard is perhaps the best known and most widely used split keyboard, but there are many others. More expensive and more ergonomic models, such as the Maltron keyboard and the Kinesis Advantage keyboard (shown in Figure A-1), use a well for each hand to put the fingers in a more comfortable typing position.

Split and Tilted Keyboards

Splitting the keys puts the hands and forearms into a more comfortable position, but both hands are still fully *pronated* (pointing downward). The next move on the ergonomic scale is to put the hands in a more neutral position by tilting the halves of the split keyboard away from each other. Various models of split and tilted keyboards

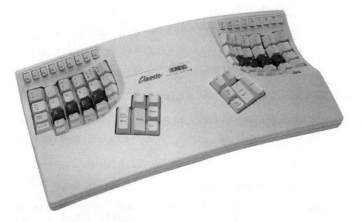

Figure A-1   *An example of a split keyboard: the Kinesis Advantage keyboard*

are available, but one of the most popular is the Maxim keyboard (shown at the top in Figure A-2) from Kinesis (**www.kinesis-ergo.com**). A more extreme split keyboard (and arguably a superergonomic keyboard) is the SafeType Ergonomic Keyboard (shown at the bottom in Figure A-2) from SafeType (**www.safetype.com**).

Figure A-2

Split and tilted keyboards like the Maxim keyboard from Kinesis (top) and the SafeType Ergonomic Keyboard (bottom) from SafeType put the hands and forearms in a more neutral and comfortable position than flat keyboards.

Superergonomic Keyboards

At this point, we move into the sphere of what you might term superergonomic keyboards. Here, things get either truly interesting or truly strange, depending on your perspective. This section presents samples of the types of keyboards you may want to examine if you need to improve your ergonomics beyond the point that split keyboards and split and tilted keyboards can deliver.

Superergonomic keyboards tackle the problem of repetitive keystrokes causing RSI in different ways: by using zero-force keys, by using different types of keys, or by not using keys at all.

FingerWorks TouchStream

The TouchStream keyboards from FingerWorks (**www.fingerworks.com**) include a custom pointing device that interprets the gestures from your hands. The TouchStream keyboards (Figure A-3 shows an example) are hard to comprehend without actually laying your hands on them and seeing what they do, but the combination of hardware and software is pretty amazing. For example, you click by tapping once with any two fingers together, and double-click by tapping once with any three fingers together. The keys themselves use what FingerWorks calls "zero-force"—you do press them, but with minimal force.

DataHand Ergonomic Keyboard

The DataHand Ergonomic Keyboard (Figure A-4) from DataHand Systems (**www.datahand.com**) is a radically different type of keyboard. In the DataHand, each finger occupies its own "well," a hole that consists of five keys: a round button to press down (as in a standard typing motion), surrounded by four

Figure A-3   *The TouchStream keyboard from FingerWorks integrates mouse and gesture support in a "zero-force" keyboard.*

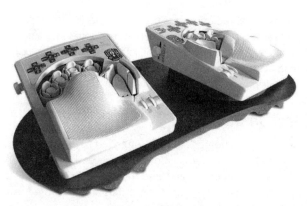

Figure A-4
The DataHand
Ergonomic
Keyboard is
strange looking
and expensive,
but its devotees
swear by it.

curved buttons, each of which you press outwards. Each thumb controls six key switches, and the keyboard supports three modes, giving the equivalent of all the keys in a regular keyboard and more.

The DataHand is available in different hand sizes and costs from $975 to $1,275 at this writing, depending on whether you go for a personal model or a programmable professional model. Its cost puts the DataHand out of the reach of most consumers; however, if your job involves huge amounts of data entry, and your company is forward-thinking enough to actively avoid repetitive-stress injury problems, *and* you've been exercising your powers of persuasion, the DataHand might seem a viable choice.

orbiTouch Keyless Keyboard

The TouchStream and DataHand keyboards have different approaches to reducing the keypresses that cause repetitive-stress problems. But if pressing the keys is the problem, clearly the solution is to get rid of the keys altogether.

You might think getting rid of the keys is a joke, but the orbiTouch Keyless Keyboard from Keybowl (**www.keybowl.com**) does just that. The orbiTouch (Figure A-5) is built around two domes that you move with your hands. Each of the domes slides to eight positions like the eight points of the compass. You type a letter by sliding

Figure A-5
Instead of keys,
the orbiTouch
Keyless Keyboard
has two domes,
each of which you
slide to any of
eight positions.

the domes to the combination of their positions that represents that character. For example, to type a T, you slide the left dome to its North position and the right dome to its East position. To type an H, you slide the left dome to its East position and the right dome to its West position. The orbiTouch has an integrated mouse, so you can keep your hands on the domes the whole time.

One-Handed Keyboards

Last in our tour of specialized keyboards come one-handed keyboard models. There are two main types of one-handed keyboards: those designed to be used on the desktop or a similar stationary surface, and those designed to be held in the hand. Not surprisingly, given how most computers are used, the former category has more occupants than the latter.

Most one-handed desktop keyboards are designed for people suffering from a permanent or temporary disability that prevents them from using both hands. For example, P.C.D. Maltron (**www.maltron.com**) makes single-handed versions of its ergonomic keyboards.

The FrogPad (shown next) from the company of the same name (**www.frogpad .com**) is an ultracompact one-handed keyboard designed for right-handed use. FrogPad has a left-handed model in the works. Unlike the Maltron single-handed keyboards, the FrogPad is primarily intended for portable and wearable computers, although it works fine with any computer that accepts USB input. Because the FrogPad has only 20 keys, you enter the less used letters, punctuation, and symbols by "chording" (holding down a key while you press another key). For example, to enter an L, you hold down [Spacebar] and press [H]. The FrogPad also supports separate modes for entering numbers and symbols. The keyboard is well thought out and comfortable to use, but learning the letter positions and the chords takes considerable effort.

The Twiddler from Handykey (**www.handykey.com**) is a handheld chording keyboard with a built-in pointing stick. The Twiddler works with either hand and connects to any computer that accepts Host USB, which makes it suitable for both desktop and handheld use. Strapped to your hand, the Twiddler feels very strange at first, and the learning curve feels precipitous. But if you put in the effort, you can get up to a decent typing speed (more than 50 words per minute) on a keyboard that you can use anywhere you have a hand free.

Index

INTERNATIONAL CONTACT INFORMATION

AUSTRALIA
McGraw-Hill Book Company
Australia Pty. Ltd.
TEL +61-2-9900-1800
FAX +61-2-9878-8881
http://www.mcgraw-hill.com.au
books-it_sydney@mcgraw-hill.com

CANADA
McGraw-Hill Ryerson Ltd.
TEL +905-430-5000
FAX +905-430-5020
http://www.mcgraw-hill.ca

GREECE, MIDDLE EAST, & AFRICA
(Excluding South Africa)
McGraw-Hill Hellas
TEL +30-210-6560-990
TEL +30-210-6560-993
TEL +30-210-6560-994
FAX +30-210-6545-525

MEXICO (Also serving Latin America)
McGraw-Hill Interamericana Editores
S.A. de C.V.
TEL +525-1500-5108
FAX +525-117-1589
http://www.mcgraw-hill.com.mx
carlos_ruiz@mcgraw-hill.com

SINGAPORE (Serving Asia)
McGraw-Hill Book Company
TEL +65-6863-1580
FAX +65-6862-3354
http://www.mcgraw-hill.com.sg
mghasia@mcgraw-hill.com

SOUTH AFRICA
McGraw-Hill South Africa
TEL +27-11-622-7512
FAX +27-11-622-9045
robyn_swanepoel@mcgraw-hill.com

SPAIN
McGraw-Hill/
Interamericana de España, S.A.U.
TEL +34-91-180-3000
FAX +34-91-372-8513
http://www.mcgraw-hill.es
professional@mcgraw-hill.es

UNITED KINGDOM, NORTHERN,
EASTERN, & CENTRAL EUROPE
McGraw-Hill Education Europe
TEL +44-1-628-502500
FAX +44-1-628-770224
http://www.mcgraw-hill.co.uk
emea_queries@mcgraw-hill.com

ALL OTHER INQUIRIES Contact:
McGraw-Hill/Osborne
TEL +1-510-420-7700
FAX +1-510-420-7703
http://www.osborne.com
omg_international@mcgraw-hill.com